PAUL BOWLES, MAGIC & MOROCCO

BY THE SAME AUTHOR

Paul Bowles: A Study of the Short Fiction. Twayne, Macmillan, New York, 1993
Al ʿAbūr ila Al ʿAbbassiya (Crossing to Abbassiya and Other Stories). Tr. by Osama Isber. Dar al Mustaqbal, Damascus, 1994
Conversations with William S. Burroughs, Editor. University Press of Mississippi, Jackson, 2000

Allen Hibbard

Paul Bowles
Magic & Morocco

Cadmus Editions
San Francisco

Paul Bowles, Magic & Morocco, copyright © 2004
by Allen Hibbard

Portfolio III, Lithograph No. 12, in Bordeauxrot, Grün
und Schwarz, 67 x 50 / 106 x 75 cm, from *Die Architektur des
Orgien Mysterien Theaters,* Volume II, copyright © 1993 by
Verlag Fred Jahn, Munich, Germany, and copyright © 2004
by Hermann Nitsch

Photo of Allen Hibbard and Paul Bowles copyright © 2004 by
Phillip Ramey

The type ornament is an architectural detail from a *ksar* in the
Bled es Siba

All rights reserved

Printed in the United States of America

Printed on acid free paper

Distributed by Publishers Group West

FIRST EDITION

Cadmus Editions
Post Office Box 126
Tiburon-Belvedere
California 94920
www.cadmus-editions.com

Hibbard, Allen
Library of Congress Control Number: 2004104141
ISBN 0-932274-61-7 *(trade edition)*
ISBN 0-932274-62-5 *(signed limited edition)*

10 9 8 7 6 5 4 3 2 1

an homage to paul
    whose magic has touched so many
dedicated to alexandra
    whose imagination is expanding
with thanks to jon
    without whom this would not be

If by your art, my dearest father, you have
Put the wild waters in this roar, allay them.
The sky, it seems, would pour down striking pitch,
But that the sea, mounting to the welkin's cheek,
Dashes out the fire.

—Miranda to Prospero, *The Tempest,* I, ii, 1-5

"I always ask leave, in the interests of science, to measure the crania of those going out there," he said. "And when they come back too?" I asked. "Oh, I never see them," he remarked, "and moreover the changes take place inside, you know." He smiled as if at some quiet joke.

— Joseph Conrad, *Heart of Darkness*

Paul Bowles first laid eyes on North Africa in 1931. The legend (which Bowles himself is largely responsible for creating and perpetuating) is that Gertrude Stein suggested he go to Morocco. He traveled through the Maghreb intermittently in the thirties then, in the late forties after the war, returned to Tangier where he lived, more or less continuously, until his death in November of 1999, at the age of 88. We need not take a measurement of Bowles's cranium to determine the profound effects of his extended residence in Morocco. His own statements and work, as well as eyewitness accounts, provide ample evidence of his engagement in and responses to Moroccan life, and the way these experiences gradually transformed him. Indeed, his identity became so closely linked to his adopted home that, for many in the West, one term (Bowles) cannot be invoked without calling to mind the other term (Morocco).

Allen Hibbard

No life in the history of American letters is comparable to Bowles's. No other American writer has committed himself so completely to a life elsewhere. Henry James's life in England seems quite timid and unadventurous when set beside Bowles's life in North Africa, surrounded by such a radically different culture whose language, history, customs, and religious beliefs lie largely beyond the ken of Western experience. Within the space between his native land and his adopted home, Bowles played, learned, exercised his imagination, and developed his personal capacities in ways he would not have otherwise.

What follows is an extended meditation on the intriguing relationship between Paul Bowles and Morocco, on the nature of those changes that took place inside him as a result of his sustained interaction with the country, its people and culture. More specifically, I am interested in how Morocco, a place where, especially when he first came there, the power of magic was yet integrally woven into the fabric of belief, enabled Bowles to develop his own imaginative powers and persona. Those who visited Bowles in Tangier often thought of him as a sort of sorcerer, magician, or guru—someone who could ever so cleverly orchestrate the forces around him simply because he understood those forces so deeply and intuitively. This essential quality lies at the heart of Bowles's unique creative genius.

In Morocco, magic is practiced more assiduously than hygiene, though indeed ecstatic dancing to music of the brotherhoods may be called a form of psychic hygiene.
—Brion Gysin, *"The Pipes of Pan"*

North Africa, from the start, stimulated certain vibrations in Bowles's psyche. The landscape became a tangible, external manifestation of his own inner being. In his autobiography, *Without Stopping*, written in the early seventies, Bowles records his initial impressions of the continent when he saw it for the first time from on board the *Imerithie II* in 1931.

> On the second day at dawn I went on deck and saw the rugged line of the mountains of Algeria ahead. Straightway I felt a great excitement; much excited; it was as if some interior mechanism had been set in motion by the sight of the approaching land. Always without formulating the concept, I had based my sense of being in the world partly on an unreasoned conviction that certain areas of the earth's surface contained more magic than others. Had anyone asked me what I meant by magic, I would probably have defined the word by calling it a secret connection between the world of nature and the consciousness

of man, a hidden but direct passage which bypassed the mind.... Like any Romantic, I had always been vaguely certain that sometime during my life I should come into a magic place which in disclosing its secrets would give me wisdom and ecstasy—perhaps even death. And now, as I stood in the wind looking at the mountains ahead, I felt the stirring of the engine within, and it was as if I were drawing close to the solution of an as-yet-unposed problem. I was incredibly happy as I watched the wall of mountains slowly take on substance, but I let the happiness wash over me and asked no questions.[1]

Penned nearly forty years after the events described, these impressions are refracted through the prism of memory, showing the enduring effect of that first encounter. Bowles recalls his feelings of exhilaration as he depicts his experience in the language of romance; he finds in reality the "other" that, up until that point, had existed only in the realm of fantasy or expectation. Moreover, that sense of romance is heightened as he realizes he has come upon a place where magic still is a live means of explaining everyday phenomena.

In *Without Stopping,* Bowles unfolds his reactions to the region as, over time, he came to know its contours more intimately. It was, for him, a place of novelty, surprise, and magic. The sharp sense of difference energized him, excited his curiosity. He took it all in much like an anthropologist, watching attentively—with amusement, amazement,

Paul Bowles, Magic & Morocco

incredulity, perplexity—as he sought to understand new patterns and behaviors. The desire to understand this wholly unfamiliar culture, to whatever extent possible, accounts in large part for his sustained fascination with Morocco. How to come to know an other so seemingly different from one's self? This metaphysical challenge was but a limit case, a symbol or metonym, for any connection between humans.

Already I have cited the passage describing Bowles's first glimpse of North Africa, from on board ship. Later, in Tetuan, his third stop, after Oran and Ceuta, he observes the behavior of the native inhabitants, noting especially their theatricality. "Each Moroccan gave the impression of playing a part in a huge drama," he recalls, then concludes: "I knew I should never tire of watching Moroccans play their parts."[2] From Tetuan, Bowles and his traveling companion Aaron Copland went on to Tangier where, following Gertrude Stein's suggestion, they checked in at the Villa de France. Here it was the city's topography and architecture that struck a chord, created a strong appeal.

> If I said that Tangier struck me as a dream city, I should mean it in the strict sense. Its topography was rich in prototypal dream scenes: covered streets like corridors with doors opening into rooms on each side, hidden terraces high above the sea, streets consisting only of steps, dark impasses, small squares built on sloping terrain so that they looked like ballet sets

designed in false perspective, with alleys leading off in several directions; as well as the classical dream equipment of tunnels, ramparts, ruins, dungeons, and cliffs.[3]

This invocation of dream and the gothic is from the man who dedicated his first book of stories, *The Delicate Prey*, to his mother "who first read me the stories of Poe," and who earlier had attended the University of Virginia, cognizant that Poe had been there before him.[4] From Tangier, a city that historically had served as a critical point of contact between Europe (via Spain) and Morocco, Copland, Bowles and the Dutch surrealist painter Kristians Tonny set off for Fez. The further he moves toward the heart of the country, the more strongly Bowles feels the presence of magic. "Tangier had by no means prepared me for the experience of Fez, where everything was ten times stranger and bigger and brighter," he writes."I felt that at last I had left the world behind, and the resulting excitement was well-nigh unbearable."[5]

It is no wonder that Fez had such a powerful effect on Bowles. This medieval Islamic city remains a treasure to this day, a living embodiment of the past. Titus Burckhard, at the outset of his classic book *Fez: City of Islam,* calls the city "a geode of amethyst, brimful of thousands of tightly packed crystals and surrounded by a silver-green rim."[6] Another metaphor: A honeycomb composed of cells, organically connected, all a part of a living, breathing organism. Or yet another: A labyrinthine arabesque of narrow, interconnected alleys and streets. The city is an ever-moving sensory symphony

Paul Bowles, Magic & Morocco

of sounds, sights, smells: the braying of mules, clopping of hooves on stone pavement, sonorous arpeggios of the muezzin's call to prayer, the percussive hammering of brass; the aroma of baking bread, spices, mint, sandalwood wafting from doors of mosques, the pungent odors of tannery vats; bolts of fabric (reds, yellows, blues, tangerines, turquoises), baskets of all sizes and designs, exquisite mosaics, baths, arches, fountains, green tile roofs, white domes, and minarets.

Bowles returned, alone, to Fez in 1932, staying at first with a friend, Abdallah Drissi, in the old city. There he became acutely aware of the distinct separation and interplay between interior, domestic space and exterior, public space, created and maintained by architecture. Doors opened from walls lining the streets into passages leading to a central secluded, tiled, mosaic courtyard around which, on several stories, living areas and balconies were arranged. The ceiling was "meticulously carved and painted with geometric and, surprisingly, floral designs."[7] Sounds of giggling slave girls gurgled from some other part of the home. Meals miraculously appeared on platters delivered by anonymous hands. From a small window in his room, Bowles watched the swallows in the afternoon. For two weeks he was a guest, a prisoner to hospitality, kept inside at his host's insistence or for fear that should he wander off without a guide he might lose himself in the maze of narrow intertwining streets, never able to find his way back to the door he had exited.

There on that trip to Fez, after moving into a hotel, Bowles ventured out on his own and for the first time witnessed the amazing trances and rituals of brotherhoods such as the Aissaoua and Hamadcha.

> I had suspected that someday I would stumble onto a scene which would show me the pulse of the place, if not the exposed, beating heart of its magic, but it was a tremendous surprise to find it first in the open street. Yet there they were, several thousand people near Bab Mahrouk, stamping, heaving, shuddering, gyrating, and chanting, all of them aware only of the overpowering need to achieve ecstasy. They stayed there all day and night; I could hear the drums from my room, and during the night they grew louder. The next morning the mob was at Bab Dekaken, just outside the hotel. Then I realized that it was a procession, moving at the rate of approximately a hundred feet an hour, with such extreme slowness that as one watched no visible progress was made. Along the edges of the phalanx there were women in trance; pink and white froth bubbled from their mouths; small shrieks accompanied their spastic motions. When someone lost consciousness entirely and fell, he was dragged inside the wall of onlookers... Here for the first time I was made aware that a human being is not an entity and that his interpretation of exterior phenomena is meaningless unless it is shared by the other members of this cultural group. A bromide, but

Paul Bowles, Magic & Morocco

one that had escaped me until then. [8]

Here was something wholly unlike anything he had ever seen in New York or Western Europe.

So strong were the impressions of these first trips that Bowles was continually drawn back to the Maghreb, imaginatively and literally, over the next decade. On return trips he traveled farther toward the frontiers, powerfully propelled by a drive to explore the unknown as well as an impulse to escape, the same forces that motivate so many of his fictional characters—Port in *The Sheltering Sky*, Nelson Dyar in *Let It Come Down*, the linguistics professor in "A Distant Episode," the photographer in "Tapiama." Bowles went farther south, into the Atlas Mountains and the Sahara, coming upon small, remote villages whose names themselves seemed to have been conjured by sorcerers of some imagined, fantastic world: Ouarzazte, Tinerhir, Figuig, Tarandout. In Algeria, too, he went farther and farther into the Sahara, away from civilization—to Laghouat, Ghardaia, Bou-Saada, Touggourt, and El-Oued.

And despite all the hardships imposed by sickness, horrid hotels, and difficult means of travel, Bowles preferred this nomadic life, with its constant novelty and ever-changing landscape, to a sedentary, more comfortable existence. "Had I believed that my constantly changing life, which I considered the most pleasant of all possible lives (save perhaps the same one on a slightly more generous budget), would go on indefinitely, I should not have pursued it with such fanatical ardor," he writes. "But I was aware that it could not be durable. Each day lived through on this side of the Atlantic was one more day spent outside prison."[9]

World War II and diminishing resources conspired to cut Bowles's contact with North Africa temporarily. Yet, upon the conclusion of the war, bored by life in New York, he managed to obtain an advance for a book and used the money to return to the Maghreb. Thus it was he wrote his first novel, *The Sheltering Sky,* deriving material from journeys into the Sahara, past and present.

From then on, up until his death, Bowles's connection to the Maghreb suffered only brief, periodic interruption. The charm of the place held him. On the last pages of his autobiography, written right after his wife Jane's death in the early seventies, Bowles reflects on his extended residence in Tangier, noting that he had never intended to live there permanently, that he had always expected to move on. However, "a day came when I realized with a shock that not only did the world have many more people in it than it had a short time before, but also that the hotels were less good, travel less comfortable, and places in general much less beautiful." In the face of deteriorating conditions around the globe, Tangier retained a certain appeal, for "it has been touched by fewer of the negative aspects of contemporary civilization than most cities of its size." Above all, however, it was the presence of magic and its potentialities that continually drew him back. He was under its spell.

> I relish the idea that in the night, all around me in my sleep, sorcery is burrowing its invisible tunnels in every direction, from thousands of senders to thousands of unsuspecting recipients. Spells are being cast, poison is running its course; souls are being dispossessed of parasitic pseudo-consciousness that lurk in the unguarded recess of the mind.
>
> There is drumming out there most nights. It never awakens me; I hear the drums and incorporate them into my dream, like the nightly cries of the muezzins. Even if in the dream I am in New York, the first Allah akbar! effaces the backdrop and carries whatever comes next to North Africa, and the dream goes on.[10]

Just as he hoped it might, Morocco gave him wisdom, ecstasy, and death.

In Morocco the dream-feeling envelops one at every step.
—Edith Wharton, *In Morocco*

Bowles was by no means the first traveler whose creativity was sparked and enlivened by the romance and charm of Moorish culture. The experiences of a long string of writers and artists of different nationalities and periods lie behind Bowles, paving his way.

The storied Arab past, on both sides of the Straits of Gibraltar but particularly in Andalusia, captured Washington Irving's imagination a century before Bowles's first encounter with the region. In 1829 Irving traveled to Granada where he found the Moorish spirit alive in the Alhambra, in the lingering legends that still wafted like ghosts through the Court of Lions and about the gardens of the Generalife centuries after the Spanish reconquest. The palpable air of the past, visibly and powerfully manifest in the architecture of the region—the Mosque at Cordova as well as the magnificent, lavish palace and gardens of the Alhambra in Granada, towers and forts and other ruins—infused Andalusia with its aura of magic. Irving recalls the Spanish reconquest, the defeat of Boabdil (the Moor's last sigh), portraying those events in a manner mostly sympathetic to the Moors. Legends of buried treasures left by the Moors still circulated several centuries after they had been pushed back across the Straits. "It is certain," Irving writes in *Tales of the Alhambra*, "that from time to time hoards of gold and silver coin have been accidentally dug up, after a lapse of centuries from among the ruins of Moorish fortresses and habitations, and it requires but a few facts of the kind to give birth to a thousand fictions."[11] These buried treasures, very often, according to legend, are protected by magic and can only be obtained by breaking the spell.

After introducing us to the Alhambra, Irving presents a series of legends, noting that the reader "must not expect here the same laws of probability that govern common-place scenes and every-day life," and "must remember that he treads the halls of an enchanted palace and all is 'haunted ground.'"[12] The tales Irving tells feature princesses, romance, lust, tyrannical power, and magic—the stuff of *The Arabian Nights*. In "The Legend of the Arabian Astrologer," for instance, a Moorish King (Aben Habuz) turns to an old Arab with knowledge of ancient Egyptian ways and skilled in the arts of magic, particularly "the mystery of the Talisman of Borsa," for help in protecting Granada from its enemies. The King sets up a tower "on the brow of the Albaicín," which serves as the base for the magician's operations. On a chessboard he arranges "a mimic army of horse and foot, with the effigy of the potentate that ruled in that direction, all carved of wood. To each of these tables there was a small lance, no bigger than a bodkin, on which were engraved certain

Chaldaic characters."[13] A bronze figure of a Moorish horseman was fixed, on a pivot, to the top of the tower like a weathervane, and it would turn to indicate the direction of any imminent attack. The battle, then, would be enacted on the chessboard, resulting in actual slaughter of invading armies.

Stories such as these, in the literature of his homeland, might well have worked their way into Bowles's consciousness long before he even laid eyes on Morocco. Might they not have opened him to the possibilities of enchantment, or even kindled within him a complex set of desires drawing him ineffably towards the land of the Moors?

Somewhat later in the century, just after the Civil War, the narrator of Mark Twain's parody of the travelogue, *The Innocents Abroad,* disembarks at Tangier. Like Bowles, the narrator is struck by the city's foreignness; his descriptions, a palimpsest, are written over *The Arabian Nights*:

> Tangier is a foreign land if ever there was one, and the true spirit of it can never be found in any book save *The Arabian Nights*. Here are no white men visible, yet swarms of humanity are all about us. Here is a packed and jammed city enclosed in a massive stone wall which is more than a thousand years old. All the houses nearly are one-and two-story, made of thick walls of stone, plastered outside, square as a dry-goods box, flat as a floor on top, no cornices, whitewashed all over—a crowded city of snowy

tombs! And the doors are arched with the peculiar arch we see in Moorish pictures; the floors are laid in vari-colored diamond flags; in tessellated, many-colored porcelain squares wrought in the furnaces of Fez; in red tiles and broad bricks that time cannot wear; there is no furniture in the rooms (of Jewish dwellings) save divans—what there is in Moorish ones no man may know; within their sacred walls no Christian dog can enter. And the streets are oriental—some of them three feet wide, some six, but only two that are over a dozen; a man can blockade the most of them by extending his body across them. Isn't it an oriental picture?[14]

After his brief stay in the exotic port (during which he collects enough material to fill a dozen pages), the narrator reboards *The Quaker City* and continues his journey, noting "Tangier is full of interest for one day, but after that it is a weary prison."[15] Twain's narrator is, to invoke a distinction Bowles makes in *The Sheltering Sky*, a tourist, not a traveler: "The [tourist] accepts his own civilization without question; not so the traveler, who compares it with the others, and rejects those elements he finds not to his liking."[16]

The French writer Pierre Loti who, like Bowles, roamed the world in search of exotic places, arrived in Morocco in the spring of 1889. Like Bowles, he was clearly enchanted by the place: "There is for me a magic and an indescribable charm in the mere sound of this word: Moghreb. Moghreb;

it signifies, at one and the same time, the west, the setting sun, and the hour of sunset. It designates, too, the empire of Morocco, which is the most westerly of all the countries of Islam.... Above all, it is the name of that last prayer which, from one end of the Mussulman world to the other, is said at this hour of the evening—a prayer which starts from Mecca, and, in a general prostration, is propagated in a slow trail across the whole of Africa, in measure as the sun declines—to cease only in the presence of the ocean, in those last Saharan dunes where Africa itself ends."[17]

Loti landed in Tangier, "a scattering of cubes of stone on the slope of a mountain," "its whiteness" set against "the deeper blue of the sea," beyond which lay "a silhouette of slate-coloured grey"—the coast of Spain.[18] The French writer traveled on horseback from Tangier to Fez, where he spent several weeks, then returned to Tangier. Loti notes at once how different Tangier was from the Europe he had left behind:

> How far away all at once seem the Spain in which I was this morning, the railway, the swift comfortable steamboat, the epoch in which I thought I lived! Here, it is as if a white shroud impended over everything, shutting out the sounds that exist elsewhere, stilling all the modern activities of life: the old shroud of Islam, which in a few days, no doubt, when we shall have advanced farther into this somber land, will envelop us more closely, but which even now, here

on the threshold, casts a spell upon us, freshly come, as we are, from Europe.[19]

This distance was temporal as well as spatial. Going to Morocco was like going back in time. It was a place where a medieval worldview was still intact, with an organic sense of time, unqualified and pervasive religious belief, an agricultural economy, and a feudal political system (with rival local lords and chiefs even). When Loti hears "the Arab bagpipe" it seems to sing a "hymn of ancient days."[20] While reading an article by Huysmanns "celebrating his joy of the sleeping-car; the black smoke; the promiscuousness and evil odours of the narrow cribs; above all the charms of his neighbour overhead," Loti feels "gratitude toward the Sultan of Fez, that he has not encouraged the sleeping-car in his empire, but has left us these wild pathways, where we travel on horseback in the sweep of the wind."[21]

Travel in Morocco was not easy then. "Roads there are none in Morocco, ever, anywhere," he wrote.[22] Loti and his party contended with floods and inclement weather as well as the prospect of attack from wild marauding bandits as they moved from one tribe's territory to another, for at the time no single political authority had hegemony over the region. His account of the trip includes painstaking descriptions of topography, vegetation (iris, marigolds, violets, etc.), the colorful parades of Arab horsemen, the weather, the light, the sounds, the changing colors. The thick descriptions, as well as the book's length, suggest an authority greater than the two months he spent in the country would warrant.

Loti's descriptions of his time in Fez take up the major portion of the book. There he broke with the rest of his party and took up residence in a room in a house in the old city. His impressions of the city are much like Bowles's. Fez is more "Moroccan," more "traditional," more "Islamic" than Tangier. Loti surreptitiously watches the women on the roofs from his small window, and dresses up in local garb so he can wander about the city without calling attention to himself. As thrilled as he is initially by the newness of the place—the souk, the crafts, people wrapped in burnouses, the labyrinth of narrow streets, the many gates and walls, the Jewish Mellah, the great Kairouiyin Mosque, etc.—he soon begins to feel claustrophobic, homesick even, as "the shroud of Islam" falls upon him "from all sides, enveloping me in its heavy, ancient folds, with never a corner raised to let in the air of other parts." It is "heavier to bear" than he would have believed.[23] He complains about the muddy streets and registers an uneasiness being among a people whose faith and ways are so different from his own.

Loti's impressions are clearly filtered through the lens of Orientalism. His lean, handsome, noble, nameless horsemen with their slender rifles spring from the paintings of Eugéne Delacoix. His eye is drawn to familiar Arab and Moroccan motifs: the costumes, ogive arches, arabesques, mosaics, stalactite ceilings, grand public ceremonies, the demonstrable power of the Sultan, sumptuous entertainment and feasts, sandalwood, rosewater, and the veil. What is secret, forbidden,

Paul Bowles, Magic & Morocco

inaccessible is most alluring. The space becomes magical, highly eroticized even, particularly as he goes native, wearing his caftan, thinking about what would happen to him if he were caught trespassing, going into forbidden places. One Friday, the Muslim day of prayer, Loti observes the religious activities in the mosque from his vantage outside: "From the darkness outside, from the kind of night that fills this skirting road where I am obliged to remain hidden, in doubtful security—all these forbidden things assume in my eye an air of enchantment."[24] An odd thrill accompanies the fear of being discovered, heightened by the prospect of getting away undetected.

After his arduous journey and time in the more isolated, foreign Fez, Loti is relieved to be back in Tangier which he deems "the height of civilisation, of modern refinement."[25] Things here seemed more familiar. With all the "ugly things and convenient things" he feels more at home.[26] People dress in European fashion, there are modern hotels, the mood is more open, and one could move about with a sense of greater personal safety.

At the end of his journey, however, the writer displays a decided prejudice toward the traditional, pre-modern culture he has romanticized throughout his travelogue. He would "rather be the most holy Caliph," he says, "than president of the most parliamentary, the most cultured, the most industrious of republics."[27] The most lowly camel-driver in Morocco, he posits, is better off—happier!—than a European factory worker. These conclusions he reaches, of course,

Allen Hibbard

without consulting the local residents concerning their own fate. He seems more interested in preserving Morocco to satisfy his needs than to meet theirs.

Loti ends his account with a sort of prayer:

> Oh, sombre Moghreb, do thou remain, for many a long year yet, immured impenetrable to things that are new; turn thy back on Europe and immobilise thyself in things of the past. Sleep on, sleep on, and continue the old dream, so that there may be at least one last country where men lift up their hearts in prayer. [28]

Putting aside the flowery prose and the religious content, the sentiments expressed here are ones Bowles later endorsed.

Henri Matisse arrived in Tangier early in 1912, just after the French Protectorate had been established, and checked in at the Villa de France. He was keenly aware of his predecessors' journeys. Loti's travelogue as well as the paintings and writings of Delacroix, who had been in Morocco eighty years earlier, circulated in his consciousness. The landscape between Tetuan and Tangier, the colorful costumes, the passion of Arab horsemen and their horses, and the parades supplied Delacroix with visual images that dramatized the Romantic ideals of his time. At one point, traveling on a mule near Tangier, Matisse recalled Loti's descriptions of the landscape and "was filled with extraordinary esteem for Loti as a painter."[29] Matisse, however, was determined to move away from the Orientalist modes of representation displayed by Delacroix and Loti. Those images often responded to and reinforced stereotypes of the Arab. Matisse sought another kind of truth, based on the purity of line, shape, and color. He sought to reveal a vision that was at once real and abstract, consistent with modernist sensibilities and impulses. Insofar as he was attracted to Islam, he was drawn to its aesthetics. In rugs, mosaics, fabrics, tapestries, and architectural features he found designs and patterns consonant with his vision. Matisse's imagination came alive in Tangier, much as Bowles's did. Both men readily found ways to incorporate all the elements around them into their work.

"Matisse did not travel to see places, but to see light, to restore, through a change in its quality, the freshness it had lost as a result of being seen day after day," writes Pierre Schneider. [30] The weather was awful when Matisse arrived in January, as it often is in Tangier that time of the year. He complained about rain and dark skies to his friend and fellow painter Albert Marquet, who had encouraged him to visit Morocco, and to Gertrude Stein. Yet, the weather did improve and as it did, so did Matisse's spirits. By March 1 he was writing to his friend Charles Camoin: "After fifteen days and as many nights of rain, we are enjoying fine weather and the vegetation, which is truly luxuriant. I have started to work and I am not too dissatisfied, although it is very difficult: the light is so soft, so very different from the Mediterranean." [31] He called the light "superb" and began immediately to incorporate Moroccan elements into his style. Loti had noted the same quality of light: "Although one distinguishes with extreme sharpness the slightest details of every object, the least crack in every wall, they are separated from us by a kind of luminous mist, which lends a vagueness to their bases, renders them almost vaporous. They look as if they were suspended in the air."[32]

An impressive, dazzling array of paintings, in various genres, resulted from Matisse's brief sojourns in Morocco from 1912 to 1913: Landscapes, subdued and sublime, cerulean and viridian (*Vue sur la baie de Tanger; Le marabout*); figural work featuring Moroccan subjects in local dress (*Amido; Zorah en jaune; La mulatress Fatma; Zorah debout; Le rifain debout*); works showing relationships between internal and external space, highlighting ornamental design, patterns in rugs and fabric, architectural features (*Paysage vu d'une fenêtre; Porte de la Casbah*); paintings of plants and trees that take on a flattened quality, becoming pattern as much as realistic representation (*Les acanthes; Les pervenches; La palme; Arums*).

The influence of his sojourns in Morocco was far greater than the amount of time he actually spent in the country would suggest. The trips came at a critical time in the artist's development and helped him move toward a sure, distinct, modernist signature.[33] "The trips to Morocco helped me to accomplish the necessary transition and enabled me to renew closer contact with nature than the application of a living but somewhat limited theory such as Fauvism had turned into had made possible," the artist has stated.[34]

Paul Bowles, Magic & Morocco

Matisse's experiences in Morocco, Pierre Schneider claims, served as the basis of the artist's middle period, from 1918 to 1930, marked by a return to realism and the preponderance of patterns.

The fit between place and style was perfect. There at the crossroads, where the Mediterranean meets the Atlantic, Matisse found a kind of earthly paradise.

Just a few years after Matisse's visit, Edith Wharton, traveling through Morocco in the midst of WWI, was struck by many features of the landscape and culture with which Bowles would later develop a much more intimate acquaintance and knowledge. "If one loses one's way, civilization vanishes as though it were a magic carpet rolled up by a djinn," Wharton writes in the account of her travels, *In Morocco*.[35] At the time Wharton visited Morocco, the country was as yet unscarred by the ravages of tourism. Few Europeans had gone beyond Tangier; fewer still had ventured beyond Fez. Roads and trails were not constructed to handle motorized vehicles, new on the scene and still relatively scarce. Not so long before her visit, as Loti's travelogue suggests, Western travelers would have been in peril. She attributes her safety to the presence of the French, who had subdued insurrection and brought a measure of order to the region. Wharton realized even then what Bowles later realized: The culture she was observing was threatened by modernity. "The strange survival of medieval life, of a life contemporary with the crusaders, with Saladin, even with the great days of the Caliphate of Bagdad, which now greets the astonished traveller, will gradually disappear, till at last even the mysterious auchtones of the Atlas will have folded their tents and silently stolen away," she writes.[36] It was precisely this absence of the signs of the modern that so enthralled and charmed Wharton, as it later worked on Bowles, who witnessed first-hand that transformation Wharton foresaw, frequently lamenting the passing of the old order marked by its belief in ritual and magic.

Wharton's senses are enlivened by white-robed Obi Wan Kenobi-like figures, pastoral landscapes dotted with shepherds, the occasional donkey or camel caravan, fig and olive trees, veiled women, spice-scented souks, saints' tombs, and minarets rising from a picturesque landscape. Like Twain, she reads her experience through the lens of *The Arabian Nights*. "Everything that the reader of *The Arabian Nights* expects to find is here," she says of the old city of Salé, a port from which pirates had come and gone not so long ago.[37] Her descriptions of dawn, en route from Rabat to Volubilis, echo Irving's descriptions of Andalusia and anticipate Bowles's impressions; like Loti and Matisse, she comments on the quality of light: "The light had the preternatural purity which gives a foretaste of mirage: it was the light in which magic becomes real, and which helps to understand how, to people living in such an atmosphere, the boundary between fact and dream perpetually fluctuates."[38]

While offering sharp, critical comments about the tightly controlled lives of women in Morocco, Wharton seems not to have fully comprehended the complexities of colonialism.

Paul Bowles, Magic & Morocco

She praises the French (in particular the work of her host, Lyautey) for their management of the country and, especially, for their efforts to preserve deteriorating architectural treasures. Indeed, it could be argued (not without dispute, however) that Lyautey formulated and implemented policies that preserved much that Bowles found (and was so charmed by) when he came on the scene just a decade or so after Wharton's visit.[39] Bowles, after all, entered a colonial scene that allowed him to move as he did, benefiting from the privileges bestowed almost unquestioningly on the Western pilgrim.

Why recite these narratives? Simply to place Bowles within the context of other travelers' experiences and impressions, and to suggest that he did not arrive innocently upon the scene. The mystique, magic and exoticism associated with Morocco had already been observed, depicted, and disseminated by a host of writers, artists, travelers, and ethnographers. As Edward Said argues in his now classic text *Orientalism*, the Middle East (and we might say by extention, the Maghreb) was largely created by the West. Orientalism he defines as "a system of knowledge about the Orient, an accepted grid for filtering through the Orient into Western consciousness."[40] These activities related to gathering and inscribing knowledge congeal and are promoted by a web of supporting institutions (schools, companies, government organizations, private societies and such). Orientalism, Said argues, serves political ends. As representations and knowledge of the "other" are produced through various

33

discourses and media, they take hold and become the basis upon which political decisions are made.

Anyone involved in studying or writing about the Orient, Said reminds us, is a part of a tradition and history involving "definite interests" stretching back to the times of Homer. "Everyone who writes about the Orient must locate himself vis-à-vis the Orient; translated into his text, this location includes the kind of narrative voice he adopts, the type of structure he builds, the kinds of images, themes, motifs that circulate in his text—all of which add up to deliberate ways of addressing the reader, containing the Orient, and finally, representing it or speaking in its behalf."[41] There is, thus, an intertextual dimension to Orientalism. Texts very often refer to other texts, to confirm views or gain authority: "Orientalism is after all a system for citing works and authors."[42] Consciously or not, Bowles created his own images and narratives in relation to pre-existing stories, prejudices, and expectations.

The definitive, comprehensive history of the complex historical relationship between Morocco and the West remains to be written.[43] And the debate concerning Paul Bowles's Orientalism will likely continue without resolution into the foreseeable future.[44]

In Morocco never be surprised. If you see a donkey flying, just say Allah is capable of anything.

— Moroccan saying

The discipline of anthropology, as many have noted, emerged at the historical moment when its central object of study—primitive cultures around the globe— was threatened by the inexorable, relentless sprawl of modernity. Indeed, the discipline is marked, even propelled, by a sense of mourning. Those encounters with the primitive, Edward Said insightfully writes, "provide us with the lively means of seeing our loss: as he was for the eighteenth-century writer of philosophical voyages, the primitive is a model for our imaginings of a lost plentitude."[45]

While Malinowski was off in the Trobriand Islands busily recording kinship patterns and sexual practices, another pioneering anthropologist, Edward Westermarck, was doing fieldwork and writing of his experiences in the Maghreb, long a favorite site for anthropologists in search of the bizarre, mysterious, and exotic. Westermarck made twenty-one journeys to the region over nearly three decades, between 1898 and 1926, just prior to Bowles's arrival on the scene. Of his numerous books pertaining to Morocco, the most relevant to our purposes is his classic study *Ritual and Belief in Morocco.* In Morocco Westermarck found superstition alive and magic an accepted feature of everyday life. Invoking Frazer's distinction between religion and magic, Westermarck notes that magic "deals with 'impersonal forces,' and aims at control or constraint, not conciliation. ... [I]t assumes that all personal beings, whether human or divine, are in the last resort 'subject to those impersonal forces which control all things,' to 'the operation of immutable laws acting mechanically.'"[46] A force generated by particular individuals, magic is thus primarily antisocial, while religion, a force generated and sustained within groups, is primarily social, serving a more general good. Westermarck notes the importance of magic to medieval writers such as Albertus Magnus. Its most salient qualities, he writes, are "its marvelousness, mysteriousness, occultness, uncanniness."[47] Suggesting that "the magical attitude is domineering and self-assertive," Westermarck states that "the word magician invariably suggests the idea of a person who claims to possess power and to know how to wield it in the magic art. In order to achieve his aim he may make use of spirits, but then he coerces them to submit to his will."[48]

Westermarck's two-volume work is a veritable encyclopedia of magical practices and superstitions throughout Morocco. He saw and described a land where the world of spirits existed side by side with the world of humans. Indeed his central preoccupation is with the interaction between

Paul Bowles, Magic & Morocco

these two worlds, the points at which they touch and overlap. Westermarck asserts that people's belief in those spirits gave them their existence. These *djinn* (*djinniya*, feminine) Westermarck describes as "spirits who seem to have been invented to explain strange and mysterious phenomena suggesting a volitional cause."[49] Taking any number of forms (frogs, toads, dogs, water tortoises, snakes, or human—particularly woman), but often remaining incorporeal, these *djinn* primarily inhabit subterranean spaces and seem to be enlivened by and travel through water, blood, and fire. (Butchers and murderers, hence, are especially susceptible to possession by *djinn*.) They are apt to be found congregating around springs, caves, rivers, and even the sea; thus, humans must be cautious, on guard, around those areas. They are known to wake after *'asar*, the mid-afternoon prayer, and be most potent and active beneath the veil of night.

Interaction between the human and spirit worlds takes a variety of forms. Nearly all the literature on magic admits the possibility for the abuse of supernatural powers (black magic) in the service of evil (*Shaitan*), as well as the possibility for its use to aid and benefit humans (white magic). As a general rule, *djinn* are best avoided. Some people, however, find ways of drawing upon the powers of *djinn* to work magic (place curses on enemies, make love potions, bring a person under their power, or assist them with certain tasks). Some men are even thought to be married to *djinniya*, notably one named Aicha Qandicha. "She appears as a grown-up woman with a beautiful face," Westermarck writes of this most notorious *djinniya*, "but she has also been seen with the legs of a goat or an ass, or with the legs of a woman and the body of a she-goat with pendant breasts. She is very libidinous and tries to seduce handsome young men."[50] Aicha Qandicha makes frequent appearances in other ethnographic work and, as we shall see, in Bowles's own writing.

Westermarck also catalogs various means by which to ward off or exorcise spirits who are tormenting humans: reciting verses from the Koran, seeking the aid of a sheikh or holy man, wearing amulets, going on pilgrimages to saints' tombs, following prescribed rituals, making sounds such as gunfire or playing loud music, lighting candles around the room, bathing in holy springs, or using substances distasteful to *djinn* such as salt, iron or steel, silver or brass, pitch, powders, smoke, incense, and henna.

Other anthropologists in Westermarck's time also focused their attention on the practices of magic in the Maghreb. Edmond Doutté's classic study *Magie et Religion en Afrique du Nord*, for instance, was published in 1909. An exquisite little pamphlet entitled *Pour une Enquête sur les Survivances Magico-Religieuses en Afrique du Nord*, written by Alfred Bel and published in Algiers in 1936, points to many such researches into indigenous festivals, costumes, and practices, *"de leur concept magico-religieux, de leurs croyances et de leurs moeurs."*[51] Bel submits a series of standardized questions and proposes to pull together anthropological findings from throughout the region. These attempts to collate and systematize knowledge, like those of Napoleon's

Paul Bowles, Magic & Morocco

expeditions in Egypt, seem aimed at consolidating and maintaining French hegemony. Bel's tract coincides with Bowles's wanderings in Algeria in the thirties. We might even imagine Bowles running into Bel, rather like Port's encounter with Lt. d'Armagnac, the colonial commander of the French military post at Bou Noura in *The Sheltering Sky*.

Just after Morocco became independent, the British travel writer Nina Epton toured the country and wrote about her experiences in a manner blending the two closely related genres of ethnography and travelogue. Her whole itinerary (Tetuan, Fez, Meknès, Casablanca, Salé, the Atlas region, the Sous) and narrative are structured around the intertwining themes of magic, religious pietism, and sorcery. She seeks out and tracks down holy men, shrines, meetings of Sufi brotherhoods, witches, haunted houses, magicians and sorcerers, snake charmers, legends of miracles, chronicles of superstitions, and stories of *djinn*, buried treasure, and clairvoyance. She visits the sheikh of Beni Salim and witnesses "the ecstatic dance of the Derkaua" near Ceuta. "Every one of his gestures and attitudes was easy and rhythmical," she says of the sheikh. "Sitting beside him, one shared in the harmonious ebb and flow of his spiritual breathing; it was as peaceful as listening to the tide on a calm summer day. He was one of those blessed people who are totally unencumbered."[52] Moroccan witches, she claims, "use many strange concoctions in their magical formulae."[53] One such concoction Epton describes is "moon foam" that "can make a husband faithful for life [and] cure him of impotence and make him madly passionate."[54] To procure this moon foam: "Go to the nearest cemetery when there is a new moon, and strip yourself naked before it. Fill a vase with water and place it under the moon. Now ride astride an oleander branch (not a broomstick!) and gallop round the cemetery seven times, from right to left, while reciting a special incantation."[55] She observes the *hadra* of the Aissaoua where adepts pierce their cheeks, shoulders and throats with swords, and put glowing coals in their mouths while dancing. Of the *hadra* she writes with a naive kind of rapture:

> There is a fairytale perfection about Moorish hadra that makes them satisfying to watch quite apart from one's private views on their spiritual content. The rustic performers, transformed under the influence of age-old esoteric rhythms, transcend their limited personality and slowly become imbued with a secret power. We are not really astonished to see them roll in palm fronds or pierce their flesh with knives that have lost their power to wound; they are characters in a fairy tale, beyond time and space, beyond earthly laws and logic, creating magic in themselves under the guidance of an invisible alchemist.[56]

She tells the story of a Jewish magician who (through divinations) helped a man find his stolen burnous. Fez, she finds particularly prone to magic: "Mystic and fairylike, old Fes forever oscillates between the magical and the miraculous."[57]

Paul Bowles, Magic & Morocco

In Casablanca she meets a *qabla* or midwife, a "sorceress of the proletariat" who reputedly could solve problems of fertility and sterility, and account for wayward pregnancies. One of the most potent anti-sterility drugs was "a sausage made from the flesh and testicles of a sheep sacrificed at the Aid el Kbir." [58] In the South Atlas she reports that women put dates in their vaginas for seven days in order to lure their husbands back to them. Among the Blue Men of Goulimine were magicians known for locating escaped slaves, or finding water in the desert.

As much as Epton (like Bowles) seems to delight in these primitive practices, she notices that they are waning and (again like Bowles) finds that the government, interested in modernization, seeks to suppress these manifestations of a "primitive" mindset. Her enthusiasms seem sometimes to get the best of her. The travelogue allows for—even encourages—a kind of appeal to sensationalism that strict ethnography scorns.

Contemporary anthropologists such as Clifford Geertz, Paul Rabinow and Vincent Crapanzano, following in the footsteps of Westermarck, have made Morocco the object of their study, extending, responding to, and building upon the work of their predecessor. The presence and operation of magic continually surfaces as they attempt to understand this culture. In his book on the Hamadcha, for instance, Crapanzano recounts legends of Sidi 'Ali, whose reported miracles elevated him to sainthood. As the story goes, he magically transports oil from Morocco to Mecca, blinds a woman, holds the sun stationary, turns soldiers into frogs, transports his disciple instantly from one place to another.[59] The power of legends such as these lies in the belief audiences put in them. So long as one believes in magic, all of these things are possible.

The extent to which this air of magic is imposed, projected, or created by the knowing subject is, at its deepest level, a question that lies within the realm of metaphysics. Nevertheless, the work of anthropologists relates to Bowles in a number of important ways. This strange and marvelous world described in these ethnographies is the same world Bowles inhabits and inscribes in his fiction. We can move dialectically between fiction and ethnography (neither of which, of course, can be treated as a reliable, unproblematic representation of the culture), teasing out some kind of truth. Moreover, especially in the case of Westermarck, by examining the nature of magic, superstition and belief, anthropologists provide us with a key to understanding how Bowles himself began to develop his powers as magician. What better place for him to practice and perform his tricks than in a culture that accepts magic as a legitimate means of explanation?

Another important concept taken up by anthropologists is that of *baraka*, which Clifford Geertz defines as "blessing, in the sense of divine favor."[60] *Baraka*, like magic, is part of the fabric of belief in Morocco and elsewhere in the Arab world. It is something like charisma, adhering to particular people, and is often associated with holiness. It is integrally connected to life-giving forces, with breath itself, and brings good fortune. To say someone or some place or some thing has good *baraka* is to say that there are perceived advantages in being in close proximity to that person, place, or thing, for *baraka* has a contagious quality. It can travel or rub off from its source. Geertz notes that *baraka* is associated with magic: "[I]t encloses a whole range of linked ideas: material prosperity, physical well-being, bodily satisfaction, completion, luck, plenitude, and . . . magical power." He goes on to describe it as "a talent and a capacity, a special ability—of particular individuals. Rather than electricity, the best (but still not very good) analogue for *baraka* is personal presence, force of character, moral vividness."[61]

This notion of *baraka* can easily be linked to that of the shaman, the wise man who is thought to possess extraordinary gifts and powers. In his superb study *Rites and Symbols of Initiation: The Mysteries of Birth and Rebirth,* Mircea Eliade dwells on the nature of narratives portraying such individuals. He identifies three ways by which a person can reach the status of shaman. It can be a spontaneous development of vocation, organic, unplanned and natural. The status can also be inherited. Or, it can come about as a result of a personal quest, a search. The shaman gains his power through his journeys to places far beyond those reached by the ordinary person. Eliade writes:

> The shaman learns not only the technique of dying and returning to life but also what he must do when

his soul abandons his body—and, first of all, how to orient himself in the unknown regions which he enters during his ecstasy. He learns to explore the new planes of existence disclosed by his ecstatic experiences. He knows the road to the center of the world, the hole in the sky through which he can fly up to the highest Heaven, or the aperture in the earth through which he can descend to Hell. He is forewarned of the obstacles that he will meet on his journeys, and knows how to overcome them.[62]

The shaman seeks ways to transcend the limits of body and ego, to gain entrance to the spirit world. The shaman is driven by a desire to free himself from limitations and live in a realm of ultimate freedom. Elsewhere, Eliade writes: "The shaman stands out by the fact that he has succeeded in integrating into consciousness a considerable number of experiences that, for the profane world, are reserved for dreams, madness, or post-mortem states."[63]

Both of these concepts—*baraka* and *shaman*—can be productively applied to Bowles. Over the time he spent in Morocco, he developed an aura that might be thought of as a secular kind of *baraka* that figured in his relations with those in the West and often even in his relations with Moroccans. Legends developed around him, giving him a certain mystique, a strong presence different from anything we might simply call celebrity or fame. He was often photographed against exotic backdrops. He mastered the symbols:

Paul Bowles, Magic & Morocco

leopard-skin slippers, ivory-handled cane. He ate the jaguar's heart. He created musical potions and collected assortments of perfumes and scents all with the purpose of creating just the right ambiance for a particular desired emotional state or outcome.[64] He was an alchemist of the first rank. People passing through sought him out, with the hope and expectation that his aura or *baraka* would rub off on them, bestowing on them some of the magic and genius of its source.

And, like the shaman, Bowles sought through his journeys to obtain as much knowledge and freedom as possible—freedom from moral restraint and freedom to create. That quest took him from Brooklyn to Paris, to Berlin, to the Maghreb, to Mexico, to Costa Rica, to India and Ceylon, to Thailand, and so many places between, as he moved nomadically about the globe. In the process, he sought out mentors whose talent had been recognized, such as Aaron Copland and Gertrude Stein, hoping perhaps that he would not only learn from them but that he could trade on his association with them. Bowles's autobiography *Without Stopping* reads like a who's who of modernism. Bowles seemed keenly aware of the benefits to be had from knowing the right people and dropping their names at the right moment. Not always having a great deal of real capital, he skillfully collected what the sociologist Pierre Bourdieu has called "social capital," which he spent shrewdly. Bowles was always very good at getting what he wanted. He once told me how he negotiated his needs with the needs of others. In any relationship, he noted, each person can be expected to want something from the other. When he was young, people he met often asked him to travel with them. "Of course they always wanted something from me. Usually it was sex. And the key was never to give what they wanted. And sometimes that caused problems. You had also to give them reason to believe you were worth spending time with."[65]

Knowing the right people was not enough, however, and Bowles was aware of that. He would often recount how Copland, ten years his senior (or was it Stein?), told him when he seemed to be slacking off that if you didn't work and produce something in your twenties then no one would love you in your thirties. If the magician's performance never becomes known, he will never gain a reputation as magician. A certain power is derived through the circulation of the name, attached to particular memorable or astonishing accomplishments. Paul Bowles became Paul Bowles by dint of his continuous, remarkable creative output; from that output and its recognition he derived his personal power. Virgil Thomson, in his review of *Without Stopping*, perceptively pointed to Bowles's discipline and personal charm as chief ingredients of his success: "Paul has always been so delicious in talk, games, laughter, and companionship, so unfailingly gifted for both music and letters, so assiduous in meeting his deadlines with good work, so relentless in his pursuit of authenticity."[66]

Very early in his life, Bowles began to establish his identity as a writer. At the age of sixteen he published poems in

Paul Bowles, Magic & Morocco

transition magazine, based in Paris and edited by Eugene Jolas. Not only did he experience a thrill upon this publication; the publication also linked him to other key figures in the modernist movement whose work had also been published in the magazine's pages, the likes of James Joyce, André Breton, Gertrude Stein, Paul Eluard, Allen Tate, and Francis Picabia. While he was still quite young, his poems were picked up and published in other small literary magazines such as *Tambour, This Quarter, Morada,* and *blues*, jointly edited by Charles-Henri Ford and Parker Tyler.

During his twenties, as he traveled about Europe and North Africa, Bowles's creative energies were channeled toward music and his name circulated with his compositions as they were performed. It was his fiction, however, that earned him notoriety and brought him the most attention. In the forties, stories such as "The Delicate Prey," "A Distant Episode" and "Pages From Cold Point" began to trickle out, and were published in a collection in 1950. In 1949, his first novel *The Sheltering Sky* was published and hit the bestseller list. These narratives took readers to geographic and psychic regions beyond their ordinary experiences. A few men from a Moroccan tribe castrate and rape a young man. An American linguist travels to Morocco, wanders into the night, is seized by natives, his tongue is cut out, and he lapses into madness. An American couple retreat from the ravages of WWII and Western civilization, moving from oasis to oasis. More and more, people began to ask: Who created these chilling tales? Who is this Paul Bowles?

Without a doubt, the distinctive features of Morocco, before which he stood (or around which he peered), heightened Bowles's allure, magnified his mystique. The country supplied an air of magic, and an array of powerful visual imagery and symbols. Photographs often showed Bowles wrapped in a burnous, standing beside Islamic arches or palm trees. He was a choice subject for glossy magazines like *Vanity Fair*. The vast distance separating him from America only added to the effect, as stories filtered back and legends developed. Of course, Morocco also provided him with the material for his fiction. What Lesley Chamberlain wrote of Nietzsche and Turin could well be said of Bowles and Morocco: "This was Nietzsche's place. It struck an immediate chord in his creative and physical being."[67] After stopping in Turin for a short time, Nietzsche declared, "This is the only place I can be." In Morocco, Bowles found that perfect synergy between "the place and the formula" referred to by Rimbaud in "Vagabonds."[68]

As with the shaman, Bowles's travels led him into "unknown regions" that provided possibilities for the "ecstatic experience." Quite literally Paul Bowles went alone into the desert, saw the sublime nothingness at the heart of existence, and returned to offer his testimony. The source of his creativity lay in these deepest recesses. In his essay "Baptism of Solitude," he describes that experience in the desert:

> Here, in this wholly mineral landscape lighted by stars like flares, even memory disappears; nothing is left but your own breathing and the sound of your heart beating. A strange, and by no means pleasant, process of reintegration begins inside you, and [you] have the choice of fighting against it, and insisting on remaining the person you have always been, or letting it take its course.[69]

Port Moresby in Bowles's most famous novel *The Sheltering Sky* also traveled farther and farther into the Sahara, farther and farther toward the abyss, toward the essential terror of excrement, blood and sky. He, however, unlike his author, never returns alive.

> ... *sorcery [and] magic* ... *try, by operating on matter and using mysterious processes of which neither the falseness or the efficacy can be proven, to capture a power forbidden to man.*
>
> —Baudelaire, "Le poème du hachisch," *Les paradis artificiel*

Bowles's views toward magic, in particular, toward the *djinn*, resemble those submitted by anthropologists such as Westermarck. In conversations with Ira Cohen, Bowles delineates between male and female *djnun*, noting that the Hammra seek out water and could sometimes take human form, possessing individuals. These unwanted, mischievous, or evil spirits can be exorcised by various means, such as those employed by the Hamadcha and other cults. When Cohen asks Bowles flat out whether he believed in the existence of *djinn*, Bowles replies:

> No, no. I believe in the existence of them as projected by common belief.... Obviously they don't exist outside the minds of people who believe in them. If they all believe in them, then they do exist. For them they exist, or it's as though they existed and therefore they exist. I can't believe in their objective existence, obviously.[70]

Bowles, like Westermarck, places the emphasis on belief. If people believe in these supernatural presences then—for them, at least—they are real, and that is what matters. In Morocco he saw that others can act on beliefs wholly alien to us.

The topic of magic and witchcraft was a favorite for Bowles interviewers. In a 1981 interview, Jeffrey Bailey asks Bowles what he knew about "Moroccan witchcraft." Bowles's lengthy reply reinforces what he had told Cohen:

> Witchcraft is a loaded word. To use it evokes something sinister, a regression to archaic behavior. Here it's an accepted facet of daily life, as much as the existence of bacteria is in ours. And their attitude toward it is very much the same as ours is toward infection. The possibility is always there, and one must take precautions. But in Morocco only what you'd call offensive magic is considered "witchcraft." Defensive magic, which plays the same game from the other side of the net, is holy, and can only be efficacious if it's practiced under the aegis of the Koran. If the fqih uses the magician's tricks to annul the spell cast by the magician, it doesn't necessarily follow that the fqih believes implicitly in the existence of the spell. He's there to cure the people who visit him. He acts as confessor, psychiatrist, and father image. Obviously some of the fouqqiyane must be charlatans, out to get hold of all the money they can. But the people get on to the quacks fairly fast.[71]

Bailey goes on to ask about Aicha Qandicha.

> You mean who do I think she really is? I'd say she's a vestigial Tanit. You know when a new faith takes over, the gods of the previous faith are made the personification of evil. Since she was still here in some force when Islam arrived, she had to be reckoned with. So she became this beautiful but dreaded spirit who still frequented running water and hunted men in order to ruin them. ... Not all Moroccans consider Aicha Qandicha a purely destructive spirit. Sacrifices are still made to her, just as they are to the saints. The Hamadcha leave chickens at her sacred grotto. But in general she inspires terror.[72]

A few years later, in a *Rolling Stone* interview with Michael Rogers, Bowles again talks about Aicha Qandicha. "I have a book that says, about 25 years ago, there were 35,000 men in Morocco married to her.... She appears to men ... never to women.... If you're a man, it's always late at night that she calls you, when you're walking, and it has to be by running water. With a certain amount of vegetation. She will call you from behind, and of course you know better than to turn around. She often calls you in the voice of your mother. If you turn around, you're lost, because she's the most beautiful woman in the world and once you look at her you have no power against her at all. You must never see her, keep going, and if possible, have a piece of steel in your

Paul Bowles, Magic & Morocco

hand. Anything made of steel, plus the right prayers, and so on. . . . There are several well-known husbands of Aicha Qandicha around Tangier. They walk along brooks and river beds, hoping to hear her voice—you see them wandering. ...And when they find Aicha Qandicha again, they make love to her right there, doesn't matter who's there. What you see is they're sort of screwing the ground, that's all. Children standing around, watching, laughing. Of course, then the police catch them and take them away. They don't beat them, just shut them up. Then they ship them to Ber Rechid [The Psychiatric Hospital]."[73]

Bowles also talked with Cohen about various magic potions used to effect spells. *Fasoukh*, for instance, he describes as "a purifier, a warder off of evil. At the same time, you can do evil with it if you work it backwards, against a person."[74]

Remarks such as these show that Bowles was thoroughly versed in the same kinds of rituals, beliefs, and practices anthropologists have noticed and studied. Though he may have denied believing in magic himself, it is natural to assume that some of these attitudes and beliefs seeped into a psyche steeped so long in this culture. He was, doubtless, transformed in subtle if not dramatic ways. He often spoke of magic as though it were ordinary, perfectly normal, not to be questioned. It was one of the things that made living in Morocco so interesting for him. He told, for instance, of how his chauffeur, Temsemany, believed that a *djinn* was responsible for causing an accident in which Bowles's Jaguar touring car was wrecked. Shortly after the incident, in November of 1951, Bowles wrote to Peggy Glanville Hicks describing the scene:

> Our chauffeur was attacked by a djinn while driving in the Oued ez Zitoun [in Fez]. The djinn seized the steering-wheel and jerked it out of his hand while he was shifting gears. He had announced the day before that a djinn was hovering around and wanted him to have an accident, but no one paid any attention. The car went full-speed into a stone bridge. Naturally it has to be rebuilt. I hope the next time the djinn will make him drive off a cliff—always on condition we are not in the car. One night an evil invisible woman appeared to him as we were going over the Col du Zegotta. The car skidded and spun abruptly around, so that it was facing the opposite way. He cursed her and she left .... Whatever happens, of course it was always written. The police say so, and the onlookers; it would be rash to suggest that the driver ought to have some control himself on such occasion. "Mektoub," [It was written] they say, smiling, shrugging their shoulders. 'Be' es-sahh,' ['true'] you say, trying to look as unconcerned as they.[75]

How Bowles relates this incident deserves as much attention as the incident itself. He stands aside, a seemingly dispassionate observer, describing what happened and how people responded as though it were perfectly natural, as though he himself found these supernatural explanations wholly plausible. His pose is that of the invisible spectator, the artist/anthropologist simply looking on, detached. The more bizarre, outlandish, perverse, or macabre the event, the more it enlivened Bowles's curiosity; normal, ordinary behavior held little interest for him. Tangier, a site where incredulous stories regularly were produced and circulated, was thus a perfect place for him. Bowles took those stories, ran them through the mill of his imagination, and retold them to Western audiences, ever aware of an appetite for exotic tales.

Bowles played on his position, adopting poses as the situation demanded. When supernatural explanations suited his purposes, he employed them. Perhaps the most well-known case in which Bowles spun stories laced with strong suggestions of witchery concerns the complex relationship between Bowles's wife Jane (also an amazingly talented writer) and a Moroccan woman named Cherifa, with whom Jane became obsessed. Paul offers this description of the Moroccan woman whom he had first spotted in the Grand Socco:

> She was sitting in her hanootz, a booth not high enough even to crouch in, just high enough to clear the top of her hat if she sat on the ground. It was like a little box. Outside were mountains of wheat and barley and oats that she was selling. She was dressed as a country woman with a great big hat and a red-and-white-striped blanket around her. At that

time she was very extraordinary looking, with beautiful shining black hair that fell around her head. She had a laugh like a savage. She was like a public monument, one of those beings you took a visitor to see—like the woman who sold coal under a certain tree in the Grand Socco, or the man who sold spells and potions in the church courtyard.[76]

Soon after Jane arrived in Morocco for the first time in 1948, Paul took her to the monument and apparently made introductions. (Could he have known intuitively that some chemical reaction would occur, and brought the two together simply to watch on and see what would happen?) Cherifa responded by asking Jane to have a bowl of soup with her. Gradually and with greater frequency, Jane began to hang out with what she called "the grain market group": Tetum, Zodelia, Cherifa and Quinza. She threw herself into learning Maghrebi, or *darija*, the local Arabic dialect, so she could communicate better with these women. She also spent time plotting how to cross paths with them, and spend more time in their company. Her mind was alive with romantic possibilities. Over the next eight years or so, when she was not in Europe or America, Jane persistently pursued these women of the grain market, particularly Cherifa, whom she saw as a sister. Cherifa's elusiveness, her "otherness," seemed only to fuel Jane's obsessiveness. No doubt thinking Jane well-to-do because she was American, Cherifa made demands for things, which Jane met, in hopes that her

Paul Bowles, Magic & Morocco

acquiescence would cement their relationship. First Jane bought shoes for Cherifa, then a djellaba. At one point Cherifa apparently asked Jane for a taxi. By 1955, Cherifa was demanding the Bowles's house in the Medina (where she and Jane had been living) if the relationship was to continue. Paul eventually caved in, likely hoping to rid himself of the annoyance.

The Bowles's marriage, we should bear in mind, was by no means conventional. Each retained a great deal of independence and freedom. Yet, especially on Jane's part, the traditional ideal of marriage loomed large in the background, producing certain expectations. Jane realized the conflict and articulated it in a letter to Paul, noting that he was "completely free and someone who will help me when he can, out of affection, and yet also that [he is] a husband."[77] Jane relied upon Paul—for validation, for support— more than he relied upon her. Or, at least, so it seemed. It is fair to say, I believe, that Paul did not meet Jane's emotional needs. Nor did he wish her to rely upon him for financial support. His income was often slim and sporadic. He insisted on securing the time he needed to write and compose, and sought to minimize his expenses and financial obligations.

By the mid fifties, Cherifa and Jane were spending a good deal of time together. During the same period Paul had established a strong bond with the young Moroccan painter Ahmed Yacoubi, whom he had met in Fez around the same time Jane met Cherifa. Yacoubi took a strong disliking to Cherifa. Yacoubi, perhaps as a means of exerting his power in the situation, warned Paul that he should steer clear of Cherifa because she was a witch and would seize any chance to poison him.[78]

In 1957, Jane Bowles suffered a stroke while Paul was en route home to Tangier from Ceylon. Illness plagued her from then on, periodically, until her death in Málaga, Spain on May 4, 1973. At times, Paul pinned the blame for Jane's ill health on Cherifa, suggesting black magic may have been involved. In a *Rolling Stone* interview, Michael Rogers asked Bowles about his wife's stroke. "I've heard that Mrs. Bowles's stroke was caused by some sort of Moroccan medicine," Rogers suggests. Bowles recounts that Jane's fasting (due to Ramadan), and heavy drinking likely put strains on her system. He goes on to say that their "rather evil maid" might have been responsible for the stroke. It might have been some magic potion, he hints. "This maid was a horror. We used to find packets of magic around the house. In fact, in my big plant, in the roots, she hid a magic packet. She wanted to control the household through the plant. The plant was her proxy or stooge, and she could give it orders before she left and see that they were carried out during the night. She really believed these things." Bowles described the substance as "a cloth bound up very tight and inside there were all kinds of things ... pubic hairs, dried blood, fingernails, antimony and I don't know what all. I didn't analyze it, no Moroccan would touch it, and I had to pick it up. Everyone around saying, don't touch it, don't touch it. I threw it down the toilet."

Paul Bowles, Magic & Morocco

As though swept away by this kind of rhetoric, Bowles continues to paint a portrait of a very sinister maid: "She was very hostile. She always carried a switchblade and when she saw me alone she'd bring it out—swish—a real quick draw. [Bowles gestures as with knife toward throat.] That's what you'll get, she'd say to me. She tried to put my eyes out one night. A monster, a real monster. I could show you pictures of her that would freeze you." [79]

Bowles retells and elaborates on this story other places. In a piece titled "The Cherifa Plant" in *Yesterday's Perfume*, for instance, Paul tells about this jinxed plant and how Cherifa stood in his way when he tried to remove the plant from Jane's apartment:

> "No the plant stays here," she declared. She was very firm and belligerent. Then she lunged at me with two fingers of her right hand spaced so that each would go into a different eye, and as I only had two eyes I backed up and left her there.[80]

According to Bowles, his Moroccan friend Mohammad Mrabet brought the plant up to his apartment. Like Yacoubi (and likely for many of the same reasons—jealousy, superstition, manipulation), Mrabet warned Paul of the dangers of Cherifa and her black magic. When Paul repotted the plant, he found the "strange things." "Don't touch it," his maid warned, fearful of the witchery.

The reason Cherifa wanted to keep the plant was that she was using it as a kind of informer. She would speak to it and tell it what she wanted from Jane. She believed that when she communicated her orders through the leaves of the plant, her words went in the roots. Cherifa spent a lot of time every night on her knees beside Jane whispering into her ear when she slept, saying things like "I need 50,000 francs tomorrow morning first thing." Of course Jane would have it in her mind when she woke up and it worked every time.[81]

Cherifa reputedly began working her magic not long before Jane had her stroke. After her stroke, doctors recommended she stay away from Cherifa, but that was the last thing Jane wanted to do. "Cherifa mixed up the medicines and made her worse," Paul writes.

I asked the doctor whether she felt that Jane's state was due to having imbibed something that Cherifa might have concocted and she said, "It's quite possible. I've been practicing medicine for eighteen years in Morocco and I've seen many analogous cases, so I don't put it beyond possibility. The important thing is to get her away from Cherifa, now."[82]

Paul stops short of blaming Cherifa for Jane's death, but not before casting aspersions on the woman's motives.

Paul Bowles, Magic & Morocco

Many of Bowles's friends have rejected the notion that Cherifa or any kind of magic or poisoning had anything to do with Jane's failing health. Edouard Roditi, for instance, has said: "Cherifa certainly did not poison Jane. No, in my opinion Jane destroyed herself. She drank to the point of being an alcoholic, and finally, drank herself into a stroke."[83] And Buffie Johnson noted that Paul would "rather call it magic, but that wasn't it. . . . Jane was a very delicate little creature. Her body just finally couldn't stand the mistreatment. All those years of drinking too much finally caught up with her."[84] Bowles himself, at times, used more scientific language to describe Jane's problems. To Virgil Thomson he wrote, just after returning to Tangier from London where Jane had been examined by doctors, that she "had what has variously been described as a 'syndrome confusionnel,' a 'spasme cérébral,' a 'small bleed,' a 'microlésion' and a 'gros accident cérébral.' Whatever it was it resulted in temporary amnesia and a permanent loss of one half of the visual field."[85]

It's hard to tell exactly what Paul believed. It's possible to conceive that he was himself conflicted, that given his intense and sustained contact with Morocco, he did seriously entertain the possibility of black magic while at the same time retaining his more analytic, Western mindset. It is also possible, as some have suspected, that he used these stories as a kind of smoke screen, to avert any blame himself. He used magic to suit his own purposes.

It was quite common, we should note, for Moroccan men to believe women poisoned them. The anthropologist Vincent

Crapanzano records this conversation with his Moroccan informer Tuhami:

> —Many Moroccans are poisoned—by women.
> —Why?
> —To get what they want. There are women who have no money and poison their husbands to get their money.
> —What can the husband do?
> —Poisoned people never know they are poisoned. They think they are just sick.
> —How do they find out?
> —There are people who can tell them because they themselves have been poisoned; they can see it in others.[86]

Bowles, too, brought up cases where men suspected that their wives had poisoned them. In "The Rif, to Music," for example, he recounts the story of Mohammed Larbi who believed his father's youngest wife poisoned him. While eating, he discovered a thread that had been used to enclose within the meat a pocket of suspicious ingredients—powders, pubic hairs, pulverized fingernails and excrement from bats, mice, lizards, and owls. "Every Moroccan male has a horror of tseuheur," Bowles writes.[87] All of these stories lie behind and inform ones he told about Jane and Cherifa.

Regardless of whether or not Bowles believed Cherifa poisoned his wife, or whether or not he expects us to believe his version of the story, he clearly maintains control over the story. He is the manipulator of stories par excellence. He understands how they are made, how they are told, and how they take hold in the listener's imagination. He creates a powerful illusion, through gesture and deed as well as through language. That's the way magic works, isn't it? If we cannot account logically for what has happened, if the person performing the trick has so skillfully concealed his art, then we call it magic. If we can see through it, it is a hoax and the performer loses all credibility, for his power depends on concealment.

The story of Jane and Cherifa has circulated widely, taking on the character of legend. It experiences a unique incarnation in Brion Gysin's *The Last Museum*.[88] Quite recently it surfaced once again near the end of Gore Vidal's *The Golden Age*. One character begins to relate the story of the two women, with its "particular romantic agony of the soul." When Jane tells Cherifa that she is in her will, the drama intensifies.

> Cherifa promptly turned murderess. Very Bowlesian this. Both Jane and Paul liked to set themselves up so that others could victimize them. At first, the sly Cherifa resorted to magic pills and potions. Only when they failed did she turn to that most effective killer: a tisane made with leaves of the datura tree. Cherifa offered Jane her poison-leaf tea, which Jane, love-glow in her eyes, drank. And drank.... Jane didn't

die right away. But she lost part of her vision. Then she had the first of a series of strokes that eventually landed her in a Spanish Catholic nursing home, where she died. Paul liked telling the story of Cherifa and Jane. With no moral, of course.[89]

True or not, this is the version we know, for Cherifa has seldom had a chance to tell her version to the Western audiences Bowles commands. (When she has, such as in Jennifer Baichwal's film *Let It Come Down*, she has denied any foul play.) We know her primarily through Bowles. His stories have molded her. We can assume that there was a good deal of friction between Paul and Cherifa. Neither, it seems, trusted the other. Both vied for Jane's attentions and affections. Jane thus may have been caught between the pulls of two competing magicians.

I want a magic carpet to visit the unfactoried corners of the world, the places that are not New York. If there are any left.
— Alfred Chester, *The Foot*

At the dawn of the twentieth century the great Irish poet William Butler Yeats directly addressed the subject of magic. "Barbaric people," Yeats muses in his essay entitled "Magic," must have possessed capacities to apprehend visions of the spirit world lost and no longer accessible to us moderns. A belief in scientific method, regimented educational systems, urban and suburban architecture, massive war machines, environmental degradation, a preponderance of technological gadgetry, global corporate management practices, and the structure of the modern workplace all have sharply severed us from these potentialities. Deprived of the supernatural, some have found our modern world a drab, dreary, desolate place. "Our souls that were once naked to the winds of heaven are now thickly clad, and have learned to build a house and light a fire upon its hearth, and shut-to the doors and windows," writes Yeats.[90] He sees this more ancient cosmology as providing conditions most conducive to the development of poetry and the other arts. "Have not poetry and music arisen, as it seems, out of the sounds the enchanters made to help their imagination to enchant, to charm, to bind with a spell themselves and the passers-by?"[91] Ireland in the early part of the 20th century, particularly rural Ireland, like Morocco, was a land rich with folklore, legend, myth, music-making, and storytelling. Like Morocco, too, it was writhing in the yoke of colonial rule. Given their cultural, historical, and geographic circumstances, both countries perhaps have experienced more acutely the assault of modernity, which threatened to radically alter all aspects of life—architecture, work, music, language, community, and belief. The great modern Irish writers were certainly keenly aware of what was at stake, as was Paul Bowles.

Despite his nostalgia for and pride in the past, Yeats did not look upon it without a certain degree of ambivalence. The past, with all its rich legendry and charm, held out immense possibilities for a sense of belonging and continuity; yet at the same time it could be an enormous burden, a heavy weight, a stagnant force that held societies back. The traditional was often associated with superstition, intolerance, and moral inflexibility. This, then, is a central tension in the modern period: a longing for a simpler past often manifest in a powerful fascination with the primitive, coupled with an equally powerful desire not to be bound by traditional forms and tight moral constraints. "I often think I would put this belief in magic from me if I could," Yeats writes, "for I have come to see or to imagine, in men and women, in houses, in handicrafts, in nearly all sights and sounds, a certain evil, a certain ugliness, that comes from the slow perishing through the centuries of a quality of mind that made this belief and its evidences common over the world." [92] In spite of this recognition, Yeats proceeds to relate in great detail his experiences with ESP and affirms his belief in the existence of the supernatural. "We must none the less admit that invisible beings, far-wandering influences, shapes that may have floated from a hermit of the wilderness, brood over council-chambers and studies and battle-fields."[93]

Perhaps no other modern personality is more strongly linked to the theory and practice of magic than Aleister Crowley (1875-1947), the self-anointed Beast of the Apocalypse and member of the Golden Dawn movement who dabbled in all sorts of esoteric rites and rituals, drawing from a vast range of traditions, from Tantrism, Gnosticism and Buddhism, to Freemasonry. Crowley's writings, which remain immensely popular today, take up astrology, yoga, the kabala, drugs, the *Tao Te Ching*, tarot, as well as magick (which he spelled thus to distinguish the concept from its more corrupt, pedestrian uses). In the years since his death, Crowley has achieved legendary, iconic, cult status, largely due to widespread invocations of his name and use of his image by contemporary performing artists. His photo appeared on the cover of The Beatle's *Sgt. Pepper's Lonely Hearts Club Band* album. He crops up in the lyrics of the Rolling Stones, Led Zeppelin, David Bowie, Darryl Hall, Sting, Ozzy Osbourne, The Clash, The Cure, and many other hardcore, punk, and industrial bands. And, Jimmy Page bought Boleskine, Crowley's castle on Loch Ness, no doubt largely because of its aura and associations with the notorious magus.

For Crowley, magic was "the science and art of causing change in conformity with will."[94] Very much like the philosophy of Friedrich Nietzsche, the aim of magic was, thus, to free the individual from social constraint and dogma, allowing him truly to be himself. As Crowley's biographer Lawrence Sutin puts it:

> Magick, for Crowley, is a way of life that takes in every facet of life. The keys to attainment within the magical tradition lie in the proper training of the human psyche itself— more specifically, in the development of the powers of will and imagination. The training of the will—which Crowley so stressed, thus placing himself squarely within that tradition—is the focusing of one's energy, one's essential being. The imagination provides, as it were, the target for this focus, by its capacity to ardently envision—and hence bring into magical being—possibilities and states beyond those of consensual reality. The will and the imagination must work synergistically. For the will, unilluminated by imagination, becomes a barren tool of earthly pursuits. And the imagination, ungoverned by a striving will, lapses into idle dreams and stupor.[95]

Not so surprisingly, Crowley's interest in magical practices took him, in 1907, to Morocco. "I was of course in paradise to be once more among Mohammedans, with their manliness, straightforwardness, subtlety and self-respect!" he wrote.[96]

Bowles's project, along with Yeats's, Crowley's, and those of early Western anthropologists, can be productively situated in the context of modern preoccupations with the primitive. Commonplace is the notion that the growing belief in science has gradually supplanted superstition and magic in the last couple of centuries. In the first half of the 20th century, a host of important figures in various fields fled the most advanced civilizations which had suffered the ravages of war and violence on an unprecedented scale, and sought solace, refuge and inspiration in warmer, distant climes, in cultures that had remained, until then, relatively remote and unscathed by the wily hand of progress. Malinowski, as already mentioned, went off to the Trobriand Islands. Gaugin headed for Tahiti where he painted barely-clad natives amidst colorful, natural tropical settings. Conrad collected material for his fiction as he traveled in Southeast Asia, Africa, and Latin America. Margaret Mead conducted her studies of adolescent young women in Samoa. Claude Lévi-Straus traveled up the Amazon into the heart of Brazil collecting myths and artifacts. (These incredible journeys he describes and meditates on in his extraordinary book *Tristes Tropiques*.) Arthur Rimbaud aborted his writing career in France and appeared in the Red Sea port of Aden, which he made his base for trading expeditions and gun-running in the African Highlands. D. H. Lawrence roamed nomadically from Sardinia to Australia, Mexico, and New Mexico. Hemingway tried to resurrect his flagging masculinity by

Allen Hibbard

hunting big game in Africa and watching bullfights in Spain. Wyndham Lewis's trip to North Africa in 1931 took him to Oran, Oujda, Fez, Marrakech, Agadir, and Tagontaft. (His writings and drawings from that trip were collected and published in 1983 by Black Sparrow, one of Bowles's key publishers, under the title *Journey into Barbary;* the term "barbary," we should recall, along with all its permutations, comes from Berber, the name given to tribes indigenous to North Africa.) The allure of the primitive is felt even in the work of those who remained in Europe or the US: in the elemental rhythms of Stravinsky's *Rite of Spring*, in Henri Rousseau's fauvist paintings of lions and jungles, in Picasso's use of African masks, in paintings by Max Weber, Marsden Hartley, and Lois Mailou Jones.[97]

Marianna Torgovnick examines these impulses in her splendid critical study *Gone Primitive,* scrutinizing their meaning.

> Primitives are like children, the tropes say. Primitives are our untamed selves, our id forces—libidinous, irrational, violent, dangerous. Primitives are mystics, in tune with nature, part of its harmonies. Primitives are free. Primitives exist at the 'lowest cultural levels'; we occupy the 'highest,é' in the metaphors of stratification and hierarchy commonly used by Malinowski and others like him.[98]

Insightfully Torgovnick suggests that "the Primitive" is one of the most salient forms of "the Other" (the Not I) in modern times, against which we define ourselves.

Though Torgovnick makes no mention of either Bowles or Westermarck, clearly the lives and investigations of both are a part of the phenomenon she examines. Malinowski, a key figure in Torgovnick's work, serves as a link to, if not a metonymic substitution for, other pioneering anthropologists such as Westermarck. In *Ritual and Belief in Morocco*, Westermarck refers to Malinowski, whose *Argonauts of the Western Pacific* appeared just four years before his own study, in a footnote, referring in particular to his acquaintance with a "savage magic." He quotes Malinowski: "The effects of magic are something superadded to all the other effects produced by human effort and by natural qualities."[99] The interesting association here is between "savage" and "magic." As we have seen, for Yeats and for Bowles, as well as for many other moderns, the sources of imagination and magic lie in earlier times or in cultures that had managed to keep modernity at bay. For Bowles, Morocco was not only a place relatively remote from the influences of strictly rational modes of thought; it was a place where the spirit world, happily, had not been extinguished or buried.

One of Bowles's favorite novels was Joseph Conrad's *Victory*, not surprisingly since the work deals with many of Bowles's own interests: expatriation, isolation, gossip, romance, moral choice, savagery, power, violence, deception, and revenge. Early on in the tale, written just prior to the outbreak of WWI, the narrator proclaims, "There are more spells than your commonplace magician ever dreamed of." [100] The enchantment of tropical islands, we presume, is one such spell. The novel fastens its attention on Axel Heyst, a Swede who has fallen under the charms of the islands in the Malayan archipelago, around Borneo and Java, and seems unable to pull himself back to a cold and friendless Europe. Would perhaps Bowles, who himself once bought an island for himself (Taprobane) off the Sri Lankan coast, have recognized something of himself in this description of Heyst?

> Heyst was not conscious of either friends or of enemies. It was the very essence of his life to be a solitary achievement, accomplished not by hermit-like withdrawal with its silence and immobility, but by a system of restless wandering, by the detachment of an impermanent dweller amongst changing scenes. In this scheme he had perceived the means of passing through life without suffering and almost without a single care in the world—invulnerable because elusive. [101]

Later, Heyst tells "Lena" (or "Alma"), a young woman he rescues from a troop of traveling musicians, that he "started off to wander about, an independent spectator" after fervently determining not to be a "cornered man." [102] Heyst wished at all costs to avoid being told what to do. His quest for ultimate freedom led him to Samburan and from there he would not budge. "Going to Europe was nearly as final as going to Heaven," we read early in the novel. "It removed a

Paul Bowles, Magic & Morocco

man from the world of hazard and adventure."[103] Of course, Heyst's position is contingent upon historical circumstance. Like Bowles, he rides the wave of colonialism, reaping the benefits bestowed upon him simply because of the color of his skin and his cultural affiliations. Heyst had been associated with the Tropical Belt Coal Company, and stayed on the premises after the company folded its operations. As a white European, he is able to do pretty much what he pleases.

The fragile, elusive nature of security is a central theme for Bowles and Conrad. As safe and invulnerable as Heyst feels on his island, outside forces conspire against him, and there is no escape. The spell is broken. Somewhat ironically, Heyst and Lena are done in not by hostile natives (who are barely seen in the novel, and when they are, lurk in the shadows, or hide behind bushes) but by fellow Europeans, greedy, unscrupulous and savage. Thus, as is so often the case in Conrad, the tables are turned, and we are asked to consider who are the real barbarians, how evil circulates, and whether we can insulate ourselves from the malevolence of outside forces.

Bowles also expressed admiration for D. H. Lawrence's fine little "travel book" *Mornings in Mexico,* another modernist text that zooms in on and seeks to capture essential qualities of the primitive experience. Lawrence vividly renders the spirit of place, a spirit created by natural landscape, weather and climate, flora and fauna, the beliefs and customs of those who live on the land. He has an eye for light and color; an ear for rhythm, music and language; a nose for

Allen Hibbard

unusual even repulsive odors and scents; and a natural curiosity about different cultural practices. The book opens somewhat comically with a rif on parrots that glides into a meditation on the various historical eras ["The Aztecs say there have been four suns and ours is the fifth."[104]] and the superior life forms associated with each. We can imagine Bowles, who himself was fascinated by parrots (and wrote about them in "All Parrots Speak," included in *Their Heads Are Green and Their Hands Are Blue*), finding amusement in Lawrence's treatment of these prehistoric birds, these vestiges of a lizard world, who shriek "with that strange penetrating, antediluvian malevolence that seems to make even the trees prick their ears."[105] Bowles would also have been able to identify with Lawrence's depictions of the natives in "The Mozo." A distance—temporal as much as geographic—lay between him and these seemingly simpler humans. The primitive lived and breathed a spirit we moderns have lost. Lawrence looks with awe on the lean, sleek, handsome, naked bodies of bathing or dancing men and women. The space between him and them is charged with longing, with desire to cross that space, to be transported magically by the other's touch.

Descriptions of Indian dances, precise and beautiful, lie at the heart of the book: "The Dance of Sprouting Corn," and "The Hopi Snake Dance" where men dance around with "poisonous snakes dangling from their mouths."[106] The Hopi dancers seek communion with the snakes because of their proximity to the sources of life—the ground, the sun. The dance is enacted to contact "the core" of that first sun, the source from which emanates both nourishment and poison, to drain and overcome the poison, to seize its vitality. Dance and song, no matter what the occasion, connect the human to the spirit, to the earth, to life-giving, regenerative forces.

The Indian, singing, sings without words or vision. Face lifted and sightless, eyes half closed and visionless, mouth open and speechless, the sounds arise in his chest, from the consciousness in the abdomen. He will tell you it is a song of a man coming home from the bear-hunt: or a song to make rain: or a song to make the corn grow: or even, quite modern, the song of the church bell on Sunday morning.

But the man coming home from the bear-hunt is any man, all men, the bear is any bear, every bear, all bear. There is no individual, isolated experience. It is the hunting, tired, triumphant demon of manhood which has won against the squint-eyed demon of all bears. The experience is generic, non-individual. It is an experience of the human blood stream, not of the mind or spirit. Hence the subtle incessant, insistent rhythm of the drum, which is pulsated like the heart, and soulless, and unescapable. Hence the strange blind unanimity of the Indian men's voices. The experience is one experience, tribal, of the bloodstream. Hence, to our ears, the absence of melody. Melody is individualized emotion, just as orchestral music is the harmonizing again of man separate, individual emotions or experiences. But the real Indian song is non-individual, and without melody. Strange, clapping, crowing, gurgling sounds, in an unseizable subtle rhythm, the rhythm of the heart in her throes: from a parted entranced mouth, from a chest powerful and free, from an abdomen where the great blood-stream surges in the dark, and surges in its own generic experiences.[107]

The motion of the dance, the rhythm of the song, the pulse of the blood are felt in Lawrence's prose. He describes and celebrates a primitive cosmology in which there are no gods in things, no gods looking on. Rather, everything is alive and anything could die at anytime. God is responsible neither for creation nor for fate. (God does not have to be killed because he does not yet exist!) "The cosmos is a great furnace, a dragon's den, where the heroes and demi-gods, men, forge themselves into being," he writes. "It is a vast and violent matrix, where souls form like diamonds in earth, under extreme pressure."[108] Naturally, man struggles to control those forces, to create conditions propitious to his own growth and survival, yet not by physically transforming the face of nature. Rather, "the Hopi sought the conquest by means of the mystic, living will that is in man, pitted against the living will of the dragon-cosmos." [109]

Like Lawrence and Conrad, Bowles sought those distant corners of the globe that had as yet received little traffic from western travelers. In the Forward to his book of travel pieces *Their Heads Are Green and Their Hands Are Blue*, Bowles announces that each time he goes to a place he has "not seen before," he hopes "it will be as different as possible from the places" he already knows.[110] The book contains pieces about his travels through South India, Turkey, and North Africa. The best, in my judgment, are those on North Africa, most of which describe trips he made in the late 1950s when, on a Rockefeller grant, he was collecting specimens of indigenous music.[111]

Like Lawrence, Bowles is drawn to primitive rituals and rhythms, which he sought to represent and preserve both in recordings and his travel writing. In "Africa Minor," for instance, he describes the ecstatic trances and dramatic head-slashing rituals of the Hamadcha cult, long an object of interest for anthropologists.

> The traveler who has been present at one of these indescribable gatherings will never forget it, although if he dislikes the sight of blood and physical suffering he may try hard to put it out of his mind. To me these spectacles are filled with great beauty, because their obvious purpose is to prove the power of the spirit over the flesh. The sight of ten or twenty thousand people actively declaring their faith, demonstrating en masse the power of that faith, can scarcely be anything but inspiring. You lie in the fire, I gash my legs and arms with a knife, he pounds a sharpened

bone into his thigh with a rock—then together, covered with ashes and blood, we sing and dance in joyous praise of the saint and the god who make it possible for us to triumph over pain, and by extension, over death itself. For the participants exhaustion and ecstasy are inseparable.[112]

In his novel *Let It Come Down*, too, Bowles incorporates vivid, stirring scenes in which the central character, Nelson Dyar, happens upon a group of Hamadcha. Dyar is pulled by the beat of the drums, drawn toward a state of ecstasy by the movement of the body, enlivened by the sight of self-laceration, the letting of blood. Indeed, this experience is one step in a gradual process whereby Dyar strips the garb of civilization and restraint, leading eventually to the chilling, tragic scene at the end of the novel when he drives a nail into the skull of his Moroccan companion.[113]

The trance music of Islamic brotherhoods such as the Hamadcha, the Aissaoua, and the Jilala, like the Indian dances described in *Mornings in Mexico*, exorcises demons and purifies the soul. Primitive practices, with their origins in Africa, have been grafted onto Islamic belief (and thus are anathema to Muslim purists). The rituals, Crapanzano notes, work as a kind of therapy and cure for maladies such as hysteria and epilepsy. They effect a certain magic, miraculously healing and driving out demons. The letting of blood connects the ritual to the deepest origins of life, rather like the Dionysian festivals in ancient Greece, or the performances of the Orgien Mysterien Theater, arranged and conducted by the contemporary Austrian composer and artist Hermann Nitsch at his Prinzendorf castle.

"The Route to Tassemsit," another piece in *Their Heads Are Green and Their Hands Are Blue,* recounts a trip Bowles made through the Grand Atlas Mountains, again in search of rare, distinctive musical specimens.[114] In a remote village he witnesses an *ahouache,* or festival of singers and dancers, which he records on tape and in writing, acutely aware that the events he observed were in danger of being subtly stamped out by the inevitable creep of modernization and external corruption (of which, ironically, he, like the anthropologist, was a visible and tangible symbol).

> The men began to play; the tempo was exaggeratedly slow. As they increased it imperceptibly, the subtle syncopations became more apparent. A man brandishing a gannega, a smaller drum with a higher pitch and an almost metallic sonority, moved into the center of the circle and started an electrifying counter-rhythmic solo. His virtuoso drumbeats showered out over the continuing basic design like machine-gun fire. There was no singing in this prelude. The drummers, shuffling their feet, began to lope forward as they played, and the circle's counterclockwise movement gathered momentum. The laughter and comments from our side of the courtyard ceased, and even the master of the palace... surrendered to the general hypnosis the drummers were striving to create.[115]

Rhythm, not melody, was, for Bowles, the basis of all music, even his own compositions. Often, when sitting with visitors in his salon at the Itesa Inmeuble in Tangier, he would commence tapping out beats, syncopated rhythms, with his fingers, whatever convenient surface—a table top, a book, the arm of a chair—serving as a drum, nodding his head slightly, in time.

Norman Mailer claimed, in *Advertisements for Myself*, that Paul Bowles "opened the world of Hip. He let in the murder, the drugs, the incest, the death of the Square (Port Moresby), the call of the orgy, the end of civilization...."[116] Bowles does indeed anticipate the counterculture of the 60s, with its drugs, sex, and rock 'n roll. Rock music, with its incessant, pounding beat and orgiastic indulgences of its star singers, signals the return of the primitive with a vengeance. It includes all the ingredients Bowles found so intoxicating in Moroccan music and rituals. A number of rock musicians, moved by the same impulses, have been inspired by Morocco and even collaborated with Moroccan musicians.[117] After touring the country, Jimi Hendrix wrote "Spanish Castle Magic" ("And though it's not in Spain, / all the same / it's a groovy name / and the wind's just right"). Jagger also traveled in Morocco and did gigues with Joujouka musicians such as Bachir Attar. Jazz musician Ornette Colman incorporates joujouka music in his marvelous, mystical album *Dancing in Your Head*. Pharoah Sanders evokes North Africa in *Tawhid and Trance of Seven Colors*. More recently Sting (who earlier wrote a song called "Tea in the

Sahara"—a direct reference to *The Sheltering Sky*) collaborated with Cheb Mami, weaving in North African melodies and voices, to produce "Desert Rose."

Sex also has a lot to do with all of this fascination with the primitive. As Torgovnick suggests, we see in the primitive "our untamed selves, our id forces." The Modern is prone to project onto the primitive an ideal of free, simple, natural, unencumbered sexual expression unavailable to him. Civilization depends upon a certain degree of repression, as Freud argues in *Civilization and Its Discontents.* The journey toward the primitive might be thought of as a means of escape, a kind of wish-fulfillment: I can do things there that I can't do here. A very seductive notion. Of course it is naive to assume that there are no restrictions, no taboos, no repression in so-called primitive societies. Rather, that free space is a liminal space, the fragile, thin membrane between cultures (perhaps not unlike the space created by pornography, or internet chat rooms, or websites devoted to sexual display) in which one can act upon one's desires outside the realm of law and surveillance. Thus, the magic: Make a wish, click your heels three times, and you're there!

At the core of D. H. Lawrence's diagnosis and critique of the modern order is the sad recognition that radical, rapid cultural changes had left so many sexual cripples in their wake. In *Psychoanalysis and the Unconscious* he writes: "Delicate, creative desire, sending forth its fine vibrations in search of the true pole of magnetic rest in another human being or beings, how it is thwarted, insulated by a whole set of india-rubber ideas and ideals and conventions, till every form of perversion and death-desire sets in! How can we escape neuroses?"[118] In *St. Mawr* Lou leaves a moribund England for vital New Mexico, trading in her pasty-faced husband for a virile young red-skinned groom. In *The Plumed Serpent* Kate, widowed, seeks a deeper connection to soul and life in Mexico, crying out to "the unknown gods to put the magic back into her life, and to save her from the dry-rot of the world's sterility."[119] In *Lady Chatterly's Lover* the central character Constance seeks sexual fulfillment elsewhere when her husband comes home from the war paralyzed from the waist down. Kit in Bowles's novel *The Sheltering Sky*, who in the last portion of the novel succumbs to the seductions of a camel driver, can also be placed within this context. These Westerners search, mostly in vain, for a natural, healthy sexuality within a culture contaminated by Christian moralism, obsessed with over-rationalization, shaken by changing sexual roles. What was needed: a way to recover some kind of unmediated, primal relation to sexuality.[120]

Lawrence sought for sexual and spiritual regeneration on an individual level as well as for a decadent modern Western culture, "an old bitch gone in the teeth" (to use a line from Pound's "Hugh Selwyn Mauberly"). Recovery of the renewing, revitalizing capacity of sex, what he calls in *Fantasia of the Unconscious* "the great magic of sex," was a key element in the regenerative project. Coition was a magical, alchemical process, a mixing of fluids that, after the act, changed those

Paul Bowles, Magic & Morocco

involved and (when conditions were propitious) produced new forms of life.

The Orient, while charged with associations connected to the primitive, carries unique connotations in the Western imagination resulting from the long, conflicted history of interactions between the two regions. A host of contemporary thinkers, including Edward Said, Malek Alloula, Ali Behdad, Greg Mullins, and Joseph Boone provide considerable insight into the cultural contexts within which Bowles is situated. For instance, Boone writes, "the geopolitical realities of the Arabic Orient become a psychic screen on which to project fantasies of illicit sexuality and unbridled excess."[121] In particular, he notes, "Morocco has ... served as a mecca for the gay and bisexual literati vacationing in North Africa—many clustered around Tangier's famous resident Paul Bowles—to say nothing of the nonliterati, those celebrities of ambiguous sexual persuasion ranging from Mick Jagger to Malcolm Forbes."[122] Prototypes for Bowles's experience lie in a number of textual and biographical precedents: Flaubert's *Letters from Egypt*, Richard Burton, Isabelle Eberhardt, Lawrence Durrell, T. E. Lawrence and—perhaps most significantly— Gide's *L'Immoralist*, a book Bowles knew well.

In his life and work Bowles responded to and played upon the erotic/exotic associations of North Africa. Whether because of some deep, residual puritanism or a sense of 19th century decorum, he always closely guarded his personal affairs, wishing to maintain a clear boundary between his private life and his public image. In fact, his mastery of the mask—by which knowledge was withheld, distance established and maintained, questions dodged and evaded —allowed him to create an illusion of omnipotence, and control events around him. Still, Bowles's close friends always knew of his interest in Arab young men, and to be sure rumors circulated. It was always assumed, however, that some things were just as well unsaid. (Once again the tension between concealing and revealing, as narrative principle, as source of power and magic.) Now that he is dead, some may be more willing to talk about his sex life.

Shortly after William S. Burroughs showed up in Tangier (on February 9, 1954, to be precise), he writes to Allen Ginsberg about Bowles. Yet an unknown figure, Burroughs seemed somewhat reticent and shy about approaching Bowles, by then well-known as the author of *The Sheltering Sky* and a collection of sinister short stories. Burroughs ascribes Bowles's unapproachability to intriguing causes. "Paul Bowles is here," he writes, "but kept in seclusion by an Arab boy who is insanely jealous and given to the practice of black magic."[123] That young Arab boy was Ahmed Yacoubi, a Moroccan painter Bowles met in Fez. (Yacoubi became the model for Bowles's rich and full depiction of Amar, the young Moroccan boy in his novel *The Spider's House*.) Though we likely will never know the precise nature of the relationship between the two, we can assume there was a magical spark of some sort. Through his friendship with Yacoubi, Bowles was able to embrace and incorporate the Other. What attracted

Bowles to Yacoubi was precisely what attracted him to Morocco—the young man's pure, uncorrupted primitive instincts, his child-like creativity. Frequently he talked and wrote about Yacoubi's mystical means of painting.

> Quickly I discovered something quite extraordinary in his method of considering his subject matter. He made next to no attempt to record the visual image of what he was drawing. Instead, he drew everything 'from the inside,' trying to express what it was like to be that person or object. This was something entirely new to me.... He began to develop his arcane procedures for injecting magic into his canvases. (He had always considered technique to be a secret which was to be protected at all costs. This attitude stayed with him all his life. No one must discover how he painted, or know what magic formulas he uttered during the act.) I never understood the source of his fanatical insistence upon secrecy. I think he believed that whoever discovered the processes involved in his technique would produce paintings identical to his. To Ahmed art was alchemy. [124]

Bowles went on to collaborate with a number of illiterate, Moroccan storytellers such as Larbi Layachi and Mohammed Mrabet. These associations, as Greg Mullins perceptively notes, were, on some level, sexually charged, connected to the complicated psycho-sexual cultural dynamics of colonialism and Orientalism.[125]

This leaves drugs, another means by which we moderns have attempted to dissolve the hard shell of ego, escape the pressures and realities of mundane lives, and cross into regions of bliss and tranquility. Charles Baudelaire, in "The Poem of Hashish," acknowledges that man, in an attempt to attain and maintain a sense of heightened imagination and happiness, has often sought "to find in physical science, in pharmacy, in the grossest liquors or the subtlest perfumes, the means to escape, if only for a few hours, from his habitation in the mire, and, as the author of 'Lazare' puts it, 'to capture Paradise at a stroke.'"[126] Those attempts, however, he goes on to say, are woefully misguided and so often go astray. The spirit "forgets, in its infatuation, that it is playing against an opponent subtler and stronger than itself; and that, if one lets the Spirit of Evil but grasp a hair of one's head, he is not slow to carry off the head itself."[127]

In the late fifties and sixties the widespread turn toward drugs was a response to the modern order similar to (and at times directly linked to) the allure of the primitive. What was Woodstock, if not the great Dionysian festival of the 20th Century, where masses of spectators sought through music, sex, and drugs to achieve another level of consciousness, to "get back to the garden"? The most popular rock music icons—Jimi Hendrix, Janis Joplin, Jim Morrison, Gracie Slick, the Stones, the Beatles, and so many others—lit up, shot up, or popped down the rabbit hole. Burroughs went

Paul Bowles, Magic & Morocco

off to Peru in search of yage. Ken Kesey and the Merry Pranksters traveled around the country stoned, on their psychedelic school bus, while Timothy Leary conducted his own LSD experiments. And Carlos Castaneda created legends of Don Juan, an Indian shaman in the southwest who had mastered the spiritual uses of hallucinogens such as peyote. The results of all this experimentation were sometimes catastrophic, as Baudelaire warned they would be. Yet, the true indictment of modern culture is not that we use drugs, but that we don't know how to use them. The job of restoring to particular drugs their magical purposes and potentialities is yet incomplete.

One reason Bowles was seen as a sort of guru by many of the Beats was that he had, as Mailer notes, been there before them. Drugs, especially those derived from marijuana, were readily available in Tangier, and Bowles was known to enjoy his kif. Like the medicine man, he knew what particular substances did and what risks were involved with each. When I was in Tangier in the late eighties I remember talking with Bowles about the use of drugs and writing. He repeated what he had said to interviewers, that he had conceived of the death scene in *The Sheltering Sky* after eating a lot of majoun. The drug opened the writer up to imaginative possibilities outside the realm of sober, rational thought. Generally, however, writing demanded a kind of control that drug-induced highs dissolved. It was best, he told me, to start writing in a sober state. One had to firmly establish the direction of the narrative. Only when you got stuck, when you ran up against a wall and didn't know where to go, should you pull out your pipe or roll a joint. Take but a puff or two, sufficient just to loosen, not immobilize, the mind. When the way becomes clear, return to the writing and follow the line as far as you can, until you hit another wall, and so on.

Bowles writes about the nature of drug-induced realities in various places. His short story "Tapiama" follows a photographer who, deep in a Latin American jungle, drinks a powerful local beverage, cumbiamba, that radically alters the workings of his mind. His fourth and last completed novel, *Up Above the World*, contains what are perhaps some of the most vivid hallucinogenic scenes in literature, as we enter the minds of characters who have been drugged. In his Preface to *A Hundred Camels in the Courtyard*, Bowles clearly describes the difference between the normal world and the "kif world":

> Moroccan kif-smokers like to speak of "two worlds," the one ruled by inexorable natural laws, and the other, the kif world, in which each person perceives "reality" according to the projections of his own essence, the state of consciousness in which the elements of the physical universe are automatically rearranged by cannabis to suit the requirements of the individual. These distorted variations in themselves generally are of scant interest to anyone but the subject at the time he is experiencing them. An intelligent smoker, nevertheless, can aid in directing

the process of deformation in such a way that the results will have value to him in his daily life. If he has faith in the accuracy of his interpretations, he will accept them as decisive, and use them to determine a subsequent plan of action. Thus, for a dedicated smoker, the passage to the "other world" is often a pilgrimage undertaken for the express purpose of oracular consultation.[128]

The four stories in this volume, all set in Morocco with no Western characters, in some way deal with the use of kif. In "Friend of the World," Salam, the main character, retreats into the kif world in order to devise plots and get his way. In "The Wind at Beni Midar," a soldier's troubles are complicated when, after smoking kif, he eats a lot of cactus fruit and loses his borrowed gun in the heap of peels. Boujemaa of "He of the Assembly," stoned, lives within his kif-induced delusions. In "The Story of Lahcen and Idir" we are told: "The difference between Lahcen and Idir was that Lahcen liked to drink and Idir smoked kif. Kif smokers want to stay quiet in their heads, and drinkers are not like that. They want to break things."[129]

Any kind of crossing, especially a crossing into the unknown—be it a primitive culture, a trance induced by hypnotic rhythms or dance, the tantalizing body of another human being, or a strange realm of consciousness opened through the use of drugs— is accompanied by risks and hazards. Burroughs aptly described Bowles as someone who maneuvered his spaceship deep into regions of the unknown without letting his hands stray from the controls. As fascinated as he was by all of these magical avenues leading to new and fresh landscapes and experiences, Paul Bowles knew the hazards, and was careful never to slide over the precipice into an abyss from which he could not return. This ability to negotiate so skillfully the treacherous, exhilarating regions alongside the abyss certainly is a source of the sorcerer's powers.

For me, a blank wall at the end of a blind alley suggests mystery, just as being in the tiny closetlike rooms of a Moslem house in the Medina evokes the magic of early childhood games, or as the sudden call to prayer of the muezzin from his minaret is a song whose music completely transforms the moment. Such reactions, I have been told, are those of a person who refuses to grow up. If that is so, it is all right with me, to whom being childlike implies having retained the full use of the imagination.

—Paul Bowles, *"The Worlds of Tangier"* [130]

Paul Bowles was predisposed to worlds of magic and sorcery. The patterns of life and belief in Morocco merely reinforced a way of being in the world that had begun to incubate and grow within him long before he encountered Morocco. As Richard F. Patteson writes in *A World Outside: The Fiction of Paul Bowles*:

> Bowles has long been fascinated with the role of sorcery in Moroccan life, but his interest in the metamorphosing powers of magic extends even further back, into his earliest childhood. The stories he told himself then, many of which he wrote down, were often tales of secret, magical places that no one else could enter. [131]

Allen Hibbard

From the time he was a young boy, an only child, Bowles began to construct imaginary worlds around him, worlds over which he could exercise a considerable degree of control, worlds which provided relief and protection from the dull and oppressive realities of life on Long Island.

At least in part, this propensity to create self-contained fictive landscapes developed as a defense against an overbearing, strict father. Repeatedly Bowles has told stories about his father's attempts to kill him when he was an infant. Whatever their validity, those stories took hold in his mind and governed his thoughts and behavior. Somewhat ironically, Paul's father, whom he loathed, may have provided the contrary without which there would have been no progression. Paul sharpened his wits and developed his talent as a means of resisting, if not triumphing over, his enemy, the figure of the oppressive father, the inflexible rule of law. His story "The Frozen Fields" displays these dynamics. Written in 1957, while Bowles was on board ship en route from Durban to Colombo, the story draws upon material from his childhood, particularly times he spent at his maternal grandparents' farm in Massachusetts. The story's opening scene shows Donald, a six-year old boy around whom all the action revolves, traveling by train with his father to spend Christmas with the grandparents. Donald etches pictures with his fingernail on the iced window beside his seat. "Stop that," his father says, and Donald's rebellion brews in silence. The story depicts Donald's attempt to carve out a life of his own making—literally and figuratively— despite his father's disapproval.[132] "I will live and flourish in spite of you!" the young boy seems to resolve. "I will make a world to stand against yours." These motivations resulted eventually in a continuous flow of creative production—musical compositions, stories, poems, novels, and translations.

Bowles's struggle to create his own autonomous space is played out in various ways throughout his early life. "One of my pastimes was the invention of lists of place-names," he recalls in *Without Stopping*. "I considered them stations on an imaginary railway, for which I would then draw a map and prepare a timetable." He goes on to tell how as a young boy, while visiting his paternal grandparents' summer home in Glenora, New York, on Lake Seneca, he actually superimposed his imaginative schemes on the landscape around him: "I printed the proper names on small slips of paper and deposited them, each one held down by a slab of shale, at what seemed the proper spot for each, along the paths in the woods."[133] His father came upon a piece of paper bearing one of the place names, Notninrivo, and brusquely confronted his son, grabbing him and asking what it all meant. The young Bowles, deeply resenting this intrusion into his interior fantasy world, refused to share its code with his father. Rather, after the discovery, Paul slipped off to gather and burn the papers on which he had written the names of these imaginary places.

> He let go of me, disgusted, having proved his point. Shortly afterward I ran up into the woods and gathered

all the station signs, starting with the one at the end of the bridge over the creek for Notninrivo and another one by a rotten tree stump a little farther along the path, this one for the town of O' Virninton. I had to destroy them in secret, for fear my father might discover the meaning of Notninrivo, which he must definitely never know. I carried the scraps of paper to a hidden cove down the shore and burned them. Then I ground the ashes into the wet shingle and piled several flat rocks on top of the spot.[134]

Somewhat less vulnerable were the imaginary worlds he created in notebooks, where he listed place-names such as Shirkingsville, 645th Street, Clifton Junction, Snakespiderville, Hiss, El Apepal, and Norpath Kay. He also invented a planet "with landmasses and seas." Ferncawland, Lanton, Zaganokword, and Araplaina he named the continents. "I drew maps of each and gave them mountain ranges, rivers, cities, and railways."[135] In these all-absorbing, solitary childhood games Bowles magically transformed the world around him. By creating a new landscape, giving names to places, and devising imaginary movement he exercised complete control over that world.

These early activities were but his first fictions. Diaries he kept when he was just ten or eleven years old contain outlines of stories in which characters "marry, divorce, remarry, have children, fall ill—many succumb to the 'Green Horror'—acquire prodigious fortunes and houses, lose them, and take injections to age thirty years at a time. They die of broken necks, influenza, and pneumonia, or their legs fall off. Forest fires devastate their communities."[136] Several years later, he recalls, he was "busy writing a collection of crime stories called 'The Snake Woman Series'":

> In each tale there was a death which, although unexpected, could be reasonably laid to natural causes. However, in each case the reader had to explain away the brief but inexplicable appearance on the scene of a woman named Volga Merna. Since the other characters were not able to remember what she looked like or what she was doing, she was never suspected. Nor was it explicitly stated she had any part in the crimes; the reader could decide. [137]

Around this time Bowles came in contact, through his Aunt Mary, with strains of theosophy and spiritualism of the sort popularized by Madame Blavatksy whose theories and ideas had earlier captured the attention of Yeats and various other literary figures. The young Bowles, thus, was aware of—and fascinated by—the possibility of mysticism, the mysterious presence of forces beyond the realm of rational explanation.

Bowles brushed against others keenly interested in magic and the supernatural, and sought ways to tap his own unconscious powers. In the thirties, during the time of his association with the Federal Theater Project, he provided music for an Orson Welles production of *Horse Eats Hay*, then a production of Marlowe's *Doctor Faustus* that made use of Welles's "repertory of magic tricks."[138] In the forties, while based in New York, Bowles worked on a translation of Sartre's *Huis Clos* (that he titled *No Exit*), ultimately directed by John Huston. During rehearsals, Huston employed hypnosis with his actors. "What I found fascinating in these experiments was the way in which they revealed the extreme malleability of the human psyche," Bowles recalled.[139]

Unlocking the door to the realm of the unconscious was key to Bowles's development as a writer. It was during World War II, while he was living in New York, that, more and more, Bowles turned to fiction as a means of self-expression. One passageway through which he gained greater access to the house of fiction was translation. Throughout his career, Bowles turned to translation as a way to exercise his writing skills, collaborate with particular people, and move interesting works of literature from one cultural scene to another. As well as the Sartre play, toward the end of the war he translated short pieces (most with a distinct surrealist flavor) by the likes of Giorgio de Chirico, Jorge Luis Borges, Francis Ponge, Ramon Sender, and André Pieyre de Mandiargues that appeared in *View*, a literary magazine edited by Charles-Henri Ford.[140] His encounters with primitive myths rekindled a desire to create his own stories. In *Without Stopping*, he explains at some length the process leading up to writing "The Scorpion" in 1945:

> I had been reading some ethnographic books with

texts from the Arapesh or from the Tarahumara given in word-for-word translation. Little by little the desire came to me to invent my own myths, adopting the point of view of the primitive mind. The only way I could devise for simulating that state was the old Surrealist method of abandoning conscious control and writing whatever words came from the pen. First, animal legends resulted from the experiments and then tales of animals disguised as "basic human" beings. One rainy Sunday I awoke late, put a thermos of coffee by my bedside, and began to write another of these myths. No one disturbed me, and I wrote until I had finished it. I read it over, called it "The Scorpion," and decided that it could be shown to others.... It was through this unexpected little gate that I crept back into the land of fiction writing.[141]

Several years later Bowles was heading back to North Africa where he began working on *The Sheltering Sky*, drawn by wistful memories of his time there in the thirties.

The course of Bowles's journey, his expatriation, took a form not unlike the classic tale of the scholar-gipsy, related by Joseph Glanvil. An Oxford student was forced for lack of means to forsake the illustrious institution of learning and take refuge among a band of wandering gypsies from whom he learned how to exercise powers of the imagination quite unknown to the academy. When his former friends from university days come upon him by chance, he dazzles them with his "supernatural" abilities.[142]

Bowles's move to Morocco substantially enhanced his power as magician in a number of ways. First, it created more distance between him and his audience. Distance is the sine qua non for magic. If the audience is too close to the performer, the tricks are more likely to be deciphered. As long as Bowles was in Morocco, he could maintain an immense appeal and sustain the allure. Bowles was not above making use of this. When others came to see him there, he was the master. He knew the culture better than others, and he could (as he so wished) use this knowledge.

Equally as important, Morocco kept him open to a childlike manner of being in the world. We might recall Torgovnick's claim that the primitive is a figure for the child. In Morocco, Bowles reclaimed his childhood, as he took in and sought to understand this new culture. This move altered his relationships with the external world, including language. Though English remained his primary language home, he stood much as a child in relation to the local Moroccan dialect. Even as he gained proficiency in the local tongue, he remained illiterate, never learning to read and write Arabic. It is not so surprising, thus, that he felt so much sympathy for illiterate Moroccans, artists such as Yacoubi and storytellers such as Mrabet and Larbi Layachi. He had little interest in the more modern aspects of Moroccan society—the world of strict calculation and reason, the world of the adult. That, after all, was what he had hoped to leave behind in New York.

Paul Bowles, Magic & Morocco

Bowles's apartment at the Itesa Inmeuble in Tangier had the air of a treehouse where the neighborhood boys could come by as the spirit moved, and escape the prying eyes of adults and parents. No topic of conversation was barred. Time passed gently, unregulated, without externally imposed pressures of having to get something done by a certain hour, or get somewhere for an appointment. Bowles, we will recall, never held a conventional job in his life. The low cost of living in Tangier allowed him to live cheaply while he wrote and composed. His creative work was serious play. He knew he had to produce and sell what he produced. Otherwise, he would have to board up the treehouse and go home.

Storytelling often assumes the aspect of magic, simultaneously banishing the existent world and creating out of airy nothing a new world that is more inhabitable.

—Richard Patteson, *A World Outside: The Fiction of Paul Bowles*

The figure of magician is certainly akin to that of fiction-writer. Both are committed to the craft of producing powerful, credible illusions. Just as the magician, with sleight of hand, dazzles on-lookers with his unfathomable transformations, the fiction writer thrills his readers with marvelous hermetic worlds hatched from his imagination. Magician and writer alike play the role of God in their circumscribed spaces, as they first create then claim credit for their work, standing aside after the act, pointing to the spectacle, as if saying, "There! See what I have made?" The audience, impressed by the performance, in awe, is left wondering "How did he pull it off?" We know it is illusion, spectacle, but we are not able to identify the series of moves that produced the effect, moves that have been carefully hidden from view. Magic, by definition, lies outside the bounds of rational explanation.

There is the magic of story, as Patteson suggests; there is also magic within stories, where supernatural causation

Paul Bowles, Magic & Morocco

supplies the logic of the narrative, such as in fairy tales. It is simply assumed, in such narratives, that magic is a viable force in the world. As a result of his stay in Morocco, as already noted, Bowles seemed at times (at least rhetorically) to have assimilated a kind of Moroccan belief in magic. Those practices of magic, and various other primitive rites and rituals, are frequently woven into the fabric of his own fiction as well as oral stories he translated. In his story "Things Gone and Things Still Here," Bowles lays out his views of the *djinn*-based universe in ways similar to his comments on magic in interviews:

> For people living in the country today the djinn is an accepted, if dreaded, concomitant of daily life. The world of djenoun [plural] is too close for comfort. Among the Moroccans it is not a question of summoning them to aid you, but simply of avoiding them. Their habitat is only a few feet below ours, and is an exact duplication of the landscape above-ground.... City people often say there are no djenoun, not any more, or in any case not in the city. In the country, where life is the same as before and where there are not many automobiles and other things containing iron, they admit that djenoun probably still exist. But they add that the automobiles will eventually drive them all away, for they can't stand the proximity of iron and steel. Then it will be only in the distant mountains and the desert where you will need to worry about them. [143]

A number of Bowles's stories show how characters act in consonance with their belief in the supernatural. In "He of the Assembly," one of the four stories in *A Hundred Camels in the Courtyard*, for instance, Ben Tajah wanders about the city of Marrakech late at night, imagining he is pursued by the she-demon Aicha Qandicha and thinking of magic potions that might rid him of her. [144]

Some of Bowles's stories contain an implicit critique of the primitive mindset that is vulnerable to the con. That which is purported to have been the result of supernatural causation turns out in fact to have been the product of clever human manipulation. Events are contrived, staged to appear as though they are miraculous, inexplicable by reason, much like the performances of the magician. Indeed, the con artist and the magician have a great deal in common. Each in his own fashion veils his means, and seeks to deceive his audience. The difference is that this is what we are expecting from the magician, while the con artist catches us off-guard, unaware of the trap being set for us until it is too late and the trap has sprung.

"The Waters of Izli" is one of a handful of Bowles tales displaying the workings of the con. The story recounts how a town is determined as the site for a saint's tomb. Two towns, Tamlat and Izli, are in contention. Tamlat has the advantage of being more prosperous and lying on higher ground. All Izli has in its favor is its spring. A means of determining the location of the tomb is decided upon. The deceased saint's stallion, the body of the saint strapped on its back, would be allowed to roam at will, and wherever he chose to stop would be the burial site. Thus, some kind of divine, indisputable logic (or pure randomness) would determine the outcome, not the intervention of human will. A clever resident of Izli, who owns land next to the spring, sees this as a golden opportunity to increase his personal wealth, and is not willing to leave the outcome to chance or providential will, however. With the aid of a local snake charmer and his own mare, he lures the saint's stallion to the spring at Izli, where the saint is then buried. As a result of the ensuing pilgrimages to the saint's tomb, the town thrives. The ruse goes undetected, so far as we know. Grounds for this kind of cynical view of the selection of saints' burial places are provided by Westermarck: "The saints of Morocco comprise not only real men and women, living or dead, but also a large number of individuals who never existed.... It is not always possible to decide whether a saint associated with a holy spot has existed or not..."[145]

Elsewhere, Westermarck writes, "Derangement of the mind is always in Morocco attributed to supernatural influence."[146] Such is the case, he says, with the *mejdoub*, "a person who is more or less out of his mind, talkative, often wearing his hair long ... but often clean in his habits."[147] Bowles builds a story, "Mejdoub", around this archetypal Maghrebi figure. The story is of a man who, after studying the ways of a real *mejdoub*, or holy maniac, pretends himself to be a *mejdoub*. The scheme works. No one suspects the imposter. An ironic kind of justice is served in the end, however, when the pseudo-*mejdoub*, taken for the real thing, is rounded up with other madmen and taken to an insane asylum, despite his protestations that he is not who he appears to be. "The months moved by. Through nights and days and nights he lived with the other madmen, and the time came when it scarcely mattered to him anymore, getting to the officials to tell them who he was. Finally he ceased thinking about it."[148] Might there be a moral to this tale? Careful who you purport to be. You might just be taken at your word! You will live the lie you invent for yourself.

Yet another story in this vein, "The Empty Amulet," vividly shows the conflict between traditional and modern values within contemporary Morocco. Marriage joins Habiba, a young woman who yet clings to superstition, and Moumen, "a young man with modern ideas" who "did not lock his bride into the house when he went out to work. On the contrary, he urged her to get to know the married women of the quarter."[149] These neighborhood women, however, make pilgrimages to the tombs and shrines of Sidi Hussein or Sidi Larbi, in search of remedies for their various maladies. To appease Habiba, Moumen has an amulet made for her. Instead of holding a real *baraka*, or inscription from the Koran with the blessings of a *sheikh*, it contains a crumpled cigarette paper. When Habiba discovers this sacrilege, this brazen form of deception, she becomes furious and asks for a divorce.

Though Bowles refrains from making any comment, this story once again hinges on duplicity that challenges traditional belief systems. One possible implication of these stories is that true magic is not possible; all that appears to be magic is but an illusion produced by tricks and clever deception. In this manner, onlookers become unwitting victims, duped and manipulated. As much as Bowles was fascinated by the idea of a world in which people believed in the supernatural, he himself, a product of the modern, scientific Western world, could not so easily abandon his skepticism toward magic. His rational, calculating mind always kicked in.

As might be expected, the pure, unquestioned presence of magic as a force in people's lives is more evident in the oral stories told by Moroccan storytellers and made available in English through Bowles's translations. In these stories magic is not a hoax; it is, rather, an accepted, natural means of explaining behavior and influencing the course of events. Chief among the Moroccan storytellers with whom Bowles collaborated is Mohammed Mrabet. The two worked to produce around a dozen volumes whose charm and appeal owe much to their fairytale quality. The operation of magic is particularly evident in *Love with a Few Hairs*, the first product of Bowles's collaboration with Mrabet, brought out in 1967. The protagonist of this short novel, a young Moroccan named Mohammed, develops an interest in a young woman named Mina. He goes to a witch in Beni Makada for a magic potion that will make her reciprocate interest and affection. For the potion, the witch says, "You'll have to bring me a piece of something she's worn, or a few of her hairs. One or the other."[150] When Mohammed returns with a few of Mina's hairs,

> She pulled out a cloth sack and began to search through it for things: packets of herbs and envelopes full of fingernails and teeth and bits of dried skin. She shook things out onto a sheet of paper, along with Mina's hairs. Then over it all she poured a powder that looked like dirt. She folded everything inside the paper and put it into a tin. A long string of words kept coming out of her mouth. She threw benzoin onto the hot coals of the brazier and she put the tin in the center of the fire, stirring it for a long time until it all had become a black powder. When it had cooled off she poured it into a paper and folded the paper into a packet.[151]

Mohammed, according to the witch's instructions, pours the powder in front of the door of Mina's house, and it has the desired effect. Mina's mother, however, is not happy with the match and seeks help from Lalla Meriam, a witch, to undo the spell. Lalla Meriam prepares a powder that Mina's mother sprinkles on the coals of the brazier in Mohammed and Mina's home. Thus spells are cast and undone. When Mohammed finally separates from Mina, in revenge she calls upon her women friends to aid in a plot to poison Mohammed, using *tsoukil*.

The stories in another volume by Mrabet, *The Chest* (1983), are likewise embued with magic, set in a world of kings, castles, and monsters. Corpses move mysteriously from grave to grave; wives try to poison their husbands; a young hero, warned by voices, kills giants and averts danger;

Paul Bowles, Magic & Morocco

mental powers create storms and winds to avenge injustice; *affrits* cast spells turning princes into birds; magic potions make resistant subjects fall in love. "Qrira" features a kif pipe that hatches diamonds, a hat that makes the wearer invisible, and a sheepskin that, when sat upon, allows one to see the future. In "The Chest" a poor man with seven daughters to feed is directed by a disembodied voice to dig under his bed. When he does so, he finds a chest full of money. The implied moral is that God rewards generosity and punishes stinginess. In "The Earth" one of the two major characters, Bhar, continually smokes "earth" and conjures visions. "Thoughts and magic," he says to his friend Jbel.[152]

These stories, set in a premodern world governed by supernatural logic, clearly show the function of magic, its transformative potential. ("Things as they are / Are changed on the blue guitar"!) One's destiny can be radically and suddenly altered, with the unexpected intervention of magic. Rigid barriers between classes can be transcended, wrongs righted, true love allowed to flourish; over night one can become rich, or marry a beautiful prince or princess. Magic seems to be used to rid the world of potential danger, to restore a sense of order, tranquility, and justice, to transform dreams into reality.

If magic is an active ingredient in the creative act of making fictive worlds, and if, as we have seen, magic is frequently at work within the fabric of a story's plot, certainly there is also the magical effect of the story on the reader. We may speak of the romance of reading, if you will. Fiction itself holds the power to transform. In and through the act of reading we leave our ordinary, mundane, dull, constrained worlds temporarily and enter, become engrossed in, imaginatively constructed, wholly self-contained worlds that extend the circumference of what we once knew, or thought possible. This is the marvelous experience we have in reading Proust. It is also the powerful effect resulting from an immersion in Bowles's fiction, heightened because of the foreign, or exotic character of those worlds. He takes us to Morocco on fiction's magic carpet.

"I have divined you well: you have become the enchanter of everyone..."
   Zarathustra to the Sorcerer in *Thus Spoke Zarathustra*,
            — Friedrich Nietzsche

Paul Bowles did not restrict his imaginative talents and skills to his musical compositions and fictions. Those who knew him often noted how skillfully he manipulated social situations. He had the capacity to orchestrate events around him, or so it seemed. He would at times seem to conspire to make things happen, then claim he had played no role whatsoever in the events: He was merely an innocent bystander. Some have even suggested he was himself spider-like, spinning webs into which he lured his prey. Indeed, Bowles was fascinated with the relationship between predator and prey. He keenly observed the habits and stratagems of poisonous spiders and scorpions as they lured their unwitting victims into death traps. These kinds of moves, too, resemble the work of the conjurer or magician. The plot is planned, the web is spun, and the predator sits aside, waiting patiently. Knowledge of the ruse, of the trick, is carefully concealed. Success depends upon careful dissembling.

An entry in Bowles's *Days: Tangier Journal, 1987-1989*

Allen Hibbard

is almost exclusively devoted to observing a particular spider. The writer seems intent upon understanding its behavior. (The predator must know the ways of his prey.)

> I have a spider whose behavior mystifies me. It's the kind of spider with tiny body and very long legs, and it spins no web. It spends its days hanging by one filament from the bottom of a marble shelf behind the door. For the past three weeks it has been going every night to hang four feet away, near the washbasin. When morning comes it returns to its corner. There are no insects for it to catch at either location, but it never misses a night. If I let anyone know of its existence it's sure to be killed. Spiders are not encouraged to live in the house. Rahma is such a poor housekeeper that the spider probably can count on months of privacy. If Mrabet or Abdelouahaid should catch sight of it, they would unthinkingly crush it. I don't know why I assume that it's entirely harmless, except that it looks nothing like the spiders that attack. These have heavier bodies and thicker legs, and are intensely, militantly black.[53]

What is most puzzling about this particular spider's behavior is that it seems not to be much interested in spinning a web and catching prey. And yet, are we to assume that it is harmless simply because "it looks nothing like the spiders that attack"?

Paul Bowles, Magic & Morocco

Bowles told another arachnid story to Raphael Aladdin Cohen (whose father Ira became closely associated with Bowles when he went to Morocco in the early sixties). In this one Bowles himself takes on the role of predator, whose prey (the spider), squirms loose from his hold.

> Paul Bowles once told me a story of how, when he was in Colombia, he pinned a large spider to the floor of his room with a hatpin.
> He assumed it would die there and dry out so that he could take it with him as a souvenir of his visit.
> The next morning he awoke horrified to find it gone.
> The spider had managed to disengage the pin and staggered off, impaled, into the night. [154]

Call it morbid curiosity or simply scientific interest: Bowles seemed especially fascinated with specimens of life that were teetering on the edge—between life and death, between sanity and madness, between vulnerability and safety, between terror and calm. He was a connoisseur of danger. When he was a young boy, signs of Bowles's sadistic streak were in evidence. In *Without Stopping* he tells about a couple of incidents involving a boy who lived next door. Around the time he was in seventh grade he had "unintentionally cut his [the boy's] head in a rock fight." [155] Thereafter their relationship was colored with a residual animosity since the boy believed Bowles had purposefully injured him. Out of guilt, Bowles tried to remain on friendly terms, but the two "always ended up fighting." Bowles seemed bothered with this state of things, and plotted a means of demonstrating his power. "There was an illogical and babyish quality about him that both infuriated and excited me, and I determined to arrange his fate and watch him undergo it."[156]

Bowles describes his scheme and its execution in detail. He turns the third floor of his house into a clubhouse, prints up announcements of a meeting, and solicits the help of two other neighbor boys— brothers— to distribute the announcements, being sure that his prey, the Linville boy, received one. There was to be an initiation, and on the night of the first meeting Bowles "casually suggested his name as the first one to be blindfolded." The boy's objections "were taken by the others to denote lack of courage and fraternal feeling; he found no sympathy. He was trying to get out of it, so they all insisted that he be the first. From then on it was not necessary for me to say anything. He was already blubbering a little when the blindfold was applied. That was perfect."

Bowles continues:

> The third floor had been left largely unfinished; there was no railing around the stairwell. My idea was to convince the boy that he was hanging out the window, when actually he was only dangling over the edge of the stairwell, and then, with proper psychological preparations, let him drop. The brothers fastened the rope around his waist, and I went and

Paul Bowles, Magic & Morocco

opened the window. He got very panicky when he heard the outdoor sounds, and they had to tie his hands behind him. When I was satisfied that he was well trussed, we lifted him off his feet. He was heavier than any of us, but we swung him around a bit and got him to the edge of the stairwell.... As soon as we let him over the edge, the rope ran through our hands hot and fast, and we had to let go. Down he went in a heap to the bottom of the stairwell. For a second there was silence, and then he began such a howling and roaring that even the grown-ups heard it and came running. Both Daddy and Mother went over him carefully and found no serious damage—only scrapes and bruises. Nevertheless, he continued to scream.[157]

Rather like an alchemist, or like Rappacini, the scientist in Hawthorne's marvelous story, Bowles often brought various elements together simply so he could observe what would happen. What will happen if I mix this substance with that? Morocco became an ideal stage for his experiments. He frequently invited people to come visit him there, perhaps because of genuine interest in company, or because he wanted to see how they would respond to this radically different culture. Any number of stories concerning Bowles's distinctive brand of hospitality in Morocco are in circulation. He could be perfectly charming. There is no doubt about it. Some visitors, however, detected a potentially sinister edge to his behavior at times. He employed various means of testing newcomers, prospective members of the club, to see if they had sufficient resources and character to play whatever games they voluntarily agreed to play—a kind of initiation ritual. Jeffrey Miller tells how Bowles, when he saw that one of his visitors, some American greenhorn, say, was not handling his kif very well, would say "Why don't you come over here, sit down, and look at this book?" He would then hand the visitor a copy of *The Eyelids of Morning*, a book devoted to Peter Beard's photographs of giant crocodiles on Lake Rudolph. The visitor could have read in the preface: "At Lake Rudolf we found one of those distant lands where dragons still roam at will, but this does not mean that it will always be so, that mankind is content to let it be. In the face of man's inexorable expansion, Lake Rudolf will one day fall and its dragons be subdued, for civilized man will not tolerate wild beasts that eat his children, his cattle, or even the fish he deems to be his. That would be regression into barbarism."[158]

Bowles would have shared the author's appraisal of the horrific consequences of modernity and growth. Crocodiles, powerful, scaly predators capable of killing man, would soon be wiped out. We had to go off and track down these frightening reptiles for the same reason Ahab was compelled to zigzag across the seas in search of the dreaded Moby Dick: This one beast embodied all of evil; if we could only be rid of it, the world would be safe. The text reads:

> For all of us, crocs symbolize evil. They are the sentinels of evil—the devil's mafia— who carry out assaults,

murders, intimidations, acts of vengeance, and other unspeakable crimes. Above all they stand for violence (often sexual violence). Huge ravening predators, armed with massive, teeth-studded jaws, strong, unrestrainable, indestructible and destructive.[159]

In the face of this, man responds with fear and rage. To subdue the threat, he uses his cunning, his intelligence, to rid the earth of this source of barbarism.

Dedicated "to all Heroes, Missionaries, and Martyrs, their perils, adventures and achievements," *Eyelids of Morning* chronicles not only the author's journey, but the explorations of the earliest white explorers to the region, such as von Hohnel, in the late 1880s. These travels into the heart of darkness, the African continent, are contemporary with Conrad's. Once again, the modern encounters the primitive, in the form of the Turkana who are flat earthists, indifferent to modern gadgetry. "Anything inexplicable in everyday terms is reckoned supernatural and explained according to the interpreter's fancy," we are told "To a Turkana, invoking some magical intervention when the rains fail or the fish refuse to hurl themselves into your net conveniently rationalizes the incomprehensible or bothersome. There is nothing like a little magic, properly concocted, for whiling away the long hours of a famine or a flood."[160]

Likely none of the visitors into whose hands Bowles placed this book would have read any of this text. Rather, it would have been the pictures that seized their eye and attention.

Allen Hibbard

The theme connecting the photos and the text is the struggle between man and crocodile, historically as well as specifically on Lake Rudolf. There is a *National Geographic* flavor to the book; a good share of pictures show barely clad black Africans alongside crocs. One of the last photos, for instance, shows several dozen Africans (mainly boys and men) holding up the skin of a croc. Many photos capture and project an air of imminent danger and terror, as predator meets prey. One photo features a large number of crocodiles cruising around in the lake, ready to devour anything living that came near. Another shows a man (Peter Beard himself, I believe) suspended on an inner tube several inches above the water, ready to take aim at one of a handful of crocodiles encircling him. (Even if you fire at a croc and it goes down into the water, you don't know if you got it or not; it could suddenly resurface, anywhere, and snap you up.) Yet another features the remains of Peace Corpsman William K. Olsen who had become the meal for crocs: a leg, bloody and mangled, in a cardboard box. Chapter 8, titled "These Serpents Slay Men and Eat Them Weeping," contains various anecdotes and drawings depicting man's unfortunate encounters with these larger, terrible beasts.

Bowles was curious to see what would happen to the poor fellow into whose hands he had placed this book. Could he handle it, or would it freak him out? If the person couldn't handle it, what was he doing here? Wicked? Devious? Perhaps. This was, after all, the man Leslie Fiedler dubbed a "pornographer of terror." And reportedly Ira Cohen said on

Paul Bowles, Magic & Morocco

one occasion, "I know Paul is guilty but I don't know what his crime is." Yet terror is but one essential dimension of human experience, one most prominent in the 20th century ("The horror, the horror"); to dismiss it would be to ignore this truth. It is perhaps in those moments we feel terror—when we feel our lives could be brutally, senselessly snuffed out in an instant, perhaps even by someone or something we have never before encountered, which for reasons of its own, carries with it enormous (perhaps even justifiable) rage and anger now directed towards us— that we feel most what it means to be alive.

Sometimes I think Gerald is God, at least a local god, or more exactly, a local demon. Africa is not the same as other continents, despite its revolutions, and Gerald has lived here so long that magic and sorcery are more part of his nature than science or the ten commandments.... If the world is illusion, why shouldn't Gerald be the cause of some of those illusions?
—Alfred Chester, *"Safari"*

Among those who were drawn into Paul Bowles's web was the young Jewish American writer Alfred Chester. The story of the relationship between Bowles and Chester dramatically demonstrates what a powerful spell Bowles could cast on those who came in contact with him. The two writers met one another in 1962 when Bowles was in New York to work on the score for Tennessee Williams's *The Milk Train Doesn't Stop Here*. Bowles was then at fifty-two already a legendary figure. The thirty-four year old Chester had published one novel (*Jamie Is My Heart's Desire*) and a handful of very fine stories, some which had won prizes. Like Bowles, he had fled New York for Paris at a young age. He had enjoyed friendships with Cynthia Ozick, Edward Field, James Broughton, James Baldwin, Mary Lee Settle, the Princess Caetani (publisher of *Botteghe Oscura*), Susan Sontag, Irene Fornes,

Paul Bowles, Magic & Morocco

and many others. In the early 1960s, while living in New York, Chester was much in demand as a critic, sparing none of his contemporaries the sting of his acerbic wit in the reviews he wrote for *Commentary, Partisan Review, Book Week,* and other magazines. Perhaps Chester was best known, however, for the flaming orange wig he had worn ever since he was a young boy, to cover a head left bald by scarlet fever. "Wig aside, Alfred Chester never looked like an ordinary person," his long-time friend, the poet Edward Field, has written, "with his tartar eyes, rosebud mouth, and almost transparent, round cheeks that seemed to join his body, avoiding a neck entirely." [161]

The two writers struck up a correspondence and when Chester voiced his dissatisfaction with life in New York, Bowles apparently suggested he come to Morocco. So serious was Bowles that he offered to finance Chester's trip, a rare gesture from a man known for his scotch ways. The Morocco veteran might have thought it would be "amusing" to see what would happen to this eccentric and bizarre character in Morocco, or he might simply have wanted the company of a bright, young, talented compatriot. The prospect of North African adventures grew in Chester's mind and he finally left for Gibraltar in the summer of 1963, paying for the trip with an advance from Random House for his collection of stories *Behold Goliath*.

In Gibraltar Alfred met up with his friends Edward Field and Neil Derrick, as planned. Chester, Field recalls, was somewhat nervous about meeting Bowles alone and thus wanted their company.[162] The three crossed the Straits by ferry to Tangier where they piled into a taxi, along with Alfred's constant canine companions, Columbine and Skoura (whom he had rescued from the Greek island of Salamis in 1959), and directly traveled the forty or fifty kilometers to Asilah, a small fishing village on the Atlantic where Paul and Jane were spending the summer. For ten days, before he got a small place of his own nearby, Alfred stayed on with the Bowleses in their lovely Indo-Arab-style, white stucco house situated along the outer wall of the fortress that guards the village and looks over the Atlantic.

Field recalls that they were all at the beach looking on as the fishing boats were being hauled in when a "very tall, handsome, bearded rather rough customer" came off a boat and strode up the beach at them "with this large fish dangling in his hand. It was pretty biblical."[163] This twenty-year old fisherman was Dris al Kasri, and Alfred fell for him hook, line, and sinker. A few days later Field and Derrick headed back to Paris.

In a letter to Edward Field dated November 4, 1989, Bowles claims credit for tutoring Dris and bringing him and Alfred together. In typical fashion, with the inquisitive detachment of a chemist mixing two volatile substances then standing back to observe, Bowles says he "was curious to see what would happen" when the two were introduced.

> ... It [is] hard to believe that Alfred never became aware that it was I who provided Dris for him. It must have

Paul Bowles, Magic & Morocco

been evident. The first time I met that young man, I decided never to have anything to do with him. He struck me as bad news, and I admit I was afraid of him. His conversation consisted solely of accounts of assaults he had made on European men, and this seemed to me a very bad sign. So, (this may sound like a non-sequitur) as soon as Alfred wrote me he was definitely coming to Morocco, I began to coach Dris on how to behave with him. We would meet for tea every afternoon in the public garden, when I'd tell him all I knew, and what I surmised, about Alfred. Reason for that behavior: I was curious to see what would happen. It turned out completely differently from the way I'd expected it to. Whatever slight violence there was came from Alfred, rather than from Dris, who seems to have been a paragon of patience.[164]

This is an extraordinary revelation. It is no wonder Chester began to see Bowles as a kind of omnipotent God, capable of manipulating and determining various elements in his life.

Bowles often noted that he had seen few Westerners come to Morocco and submerge themselves into local life so quickly and fully as did Alfred Chester. Chester's early letters from Morocco exhibit a great deal of excitement at seeing and participating in local rites and rituals. He mentions, with fascination, the circumcision ceremonies in which the young boy, traditionally dressed, is paraded around the streets on a donkey. He notes, too, the celebration of *mulad al-nabi* (the Birthday of the Prophet Mohammad), and the Hamadcha cult meetings where "they go into trances and cut their heads open with axes and rocks." Writing to Edward Field, he continues to say that "Dris's father is a leading member. He is a cherif. So is Dris. This obviously makes me a cheriffa."[165]

Chester's relationship with Bowles over the next couple of years was somewhat rocky. Chester admired Bowles's writing and stood in awe of his towering persona, yet somehow never wholly trusted him. As early as July 22, 1963, in a letter to Dennis Selby, Alfred was referring to Bowles as "monstrously possessive, an old fashioned colonial type." In a letter to Edward Field, he calls Bowles a "dried up Dr. Schweitzer" and complains of Bowles trying to control him. "He really wants to own me. He is so used to owning people and things here. He keeps saying 'they' about the Moroccans, even when he means 'he.' Like Larbi [Layachi] says something and Paul delivers a comment on 'they' to me. He is incapable of conversation. To tell the truth I loathe him."[166] And to Harriet Sohmers he writes that Paul was "kifed out of his mind most of the time, and ... terribly unhappy."[167]

Chester wins no love from Bowles when he takes the side of Larbi against his employer. When Alfred goes to borrow blankets from Paul, Paul refuses. The highly sensitive Chester took the refusal as a personal attack, a breech of faith. He also accuses Bowles of trying to come between him and Dris. Chester's paranoia is further fueled when he discovers that Bowles had written a note to Ira Cohen

Paul Bowles, Magic & Morocco

saying that he was arranging to have Chester and the British writer Norman Glass (another troublesome character) "bumped off." As much as Bowles insisted he was merely joking, Chester took him seriously and went to the American consul to complain. Another legendary incident grew up around the little literary magazine *Gnaoua* that Cohen had started up in Tangier. Chester apparently hatched some kind of blackmail scheme whereby the magazine would publish a potentially slanderous line referring to Bowles unless the writer coughed up some money. Chester claimed this was a joke, though Bowles was not amused.

Chester, who was consuming large quantities of drugs and alcohol during this time, thought he was being driven mad. Moreover, he believed Paul Bowles was largely responsible for what was happening around him. Alfred's fears and illusions were, in Alfred's mind, logically derived. "These people here," he wrote to Field, "are not like the people we've ever known. Bill Burroughs, as you know, murdered his wife. Jane's best friend Libby Holman murdered her husband... Paul and Jane are poison."[168] Chester was not content simply to sit back and accept the order of things. His personal and literary mission, seen in the marvelous masterpiece *The Exquisite Corpse* (written while he was in Morocco), was to behold the mask, rip it away, and display it openly as mask. His impulse was to find out just who the Wizard of Oz was, pull aside the curtain, and let people see the levers and gears. Chester likely became too much for Bowles to handle. Though often considered the consummate outsider,

Bowles was, in many respects, quite conservative, queerly puritanical even. The man who has written some of the most devious stories of horror and perversion has at the same time insisted upon a clear (almost Victorian) distinction between the personal and public in his own life. This social posture would have irritated Alfred, striking him as hypocritical and dishonest. As much as Paul admired the dazzling quality of Alfred's writing ("Chester examines the complex perversity of human behavior; since he is a stylistic virtuoso, his reports are varied and brilliant," Bowles wrote for use as a book blurb), he would have no truck with Alfred's erratic social behavior, bent, it sometimes seemed, simply on causing disruption in other people's lives, violating basic principles of friendship and respect.

Chester's marvelous story "Safari," about a scorpion hunt, brilliantly captures the essential nature of both central characters, casting Bowles in the role of sorcerer, mage. In the story Bowles becomes "Gerald." (In Chester's piece "The Foot," he is Peter Plate.) At the story's outset, the narrator is waiting for Gerald at a park (in Tangier, though never specified), their agreed upon place of rendezvous. When Gerald finally appears, he is wearing "chinos and a plaid shirt." By contrast, the narrator (Chester) wears clothing entirely unsuitable for the expedition: "a jacket and a tie and my narrow Italian shoes, bought three years ago at Macy's, and hardly ever worn." He admits to feeling "ridiculous" in this get up, and wonders if he should perhaps go home and change. The narrator offers this description of

Paul Bowles, Magic & Morocco

Gerald:

> At ten yards or more away, you would think he was fifteen years old, though in fact he's almost at the other end of middle age. He is small and thin like a boy, but not muscular, full of quick nervous energy, and his hair is still very blond. If there is any gray in his hair, it doesn't show.[169]

Gerald's physical features ("his hollow, pale, pale blue eyes") and mannerisms ("he drummed with his fingers on the side of the can") are unmistakably Paul's.

Gerald is prepared for the hunt. His equipment consists of a large powdered milk can and "a pair of cuticle scissors." They head off, out of town, through the surrounding suburbs toward the Drin valley, outside Tangier. The suburban homes, built by Europeans, "sit like crumbling futuristic fantasies, shuttered, chained, empty, eviscerated. Walking past, you get the feeling that people must be secretly slipping off to other planets, and that soon you will be left alone here, that you'll have the solitary run of the world along with all its antique futuristic houses."[170] The hills beyond, practically devoid of habitation, are dry and barren.

Throughout the hunt, the narrator is amazed at the tortuous distance Gerald creates between himself and his prey. "I wonder if he were really excited," Chester writes. "You can never tell with him if he really cares about anything. I don't believe he does. I think the only thing he genuinely cares about is watching things squirm. Things and people."[171] Yet, one feels at the same time a kind of grudging admiration, if not outright awe, for Bowles's aesthetic:

> As we walked, he pointed out shrubbery, grasses, and even small flowers. To me the land had looked parched, but since Gerald is extremely observant, the valley came to life. Not to [*sic*] much of a life, but a life just the same. Gerald remembers what he looks at, classifies what he sees, will recollect a plant if he comes across it. He remembers smells and colors and shapes. The world I live in has few details and practically no names, and seldom repeats itself. I see a large anonymous blur that is every day replaced by another large anonymous blur.[172]

The difference between the two men and their aesthetics is sharply drawn. Gerald is portrayed as cold, calculating and objective, while the narrator is more passionate, spontaneous, and unconstrained.

A bit ironically, however, the narrator displays the same keen powers of observation he ascribes to Gerald. The hunt is described in scrupulous detail: how Gerald enlists the help of a young Moroccan boy to accompany them on the expedition, how the scorpion's hole is located and the prey lured out with a palmetto leaf, captured and its tail snipped off with scissors. "The trick," Gerald instructs the narrator, "is to get the leaf up with the scorpion still holding the other end of it."[173] For Gerald it is all an art. When the Arab boy cuts the tail off one scorpion, Gerald exclaims with annoyance,

> "You've cut too much off."
> "No, it's better this way."
> Gerald waved his arms helplessly. "All you really need to cut off is the stinger and the poison sack just behind. Then it's perfectly harmless. You've ruined the look of it now." [174]

Six scorpions are caught in all—five by the Moroccan and one by Gerald. After the hunt Gerald offers the narrator a cigarette. "I can't smoke these days," he replies. Gerald then goes on to say that "If you surround a scorpion with a ring of fire, he'll investigate all around, and when he finds he can't escape, he'll sting himself in the back of the head. Commit suicide. Isn't that sad?" The narrator feels Gerald is talking about him, not the scorpion. Prophetic—knowing, as we do now, that Chester would find himself in the position of that scorpion, surrounded by fire (figuratively speaking), in Jerusalem, five or six years later, with no way out but death.

Gerald leaves the narrator with three scorpions, which he puts in a ventilated cardboard box. Two die within a couple of days. The other (perhaps sustained by eating the innards of the other two, the narrator speculates) lives and grows strong. In the end, the narrator returns to the scene of the scorpion's capture and releases it.

The extent to which Chester was pre-occupied with Bowles, and held him in such awe is felt in the narrator's unspoken commentary, a portion of which serves as the epigram for this section. Chester thus saw Bowles as magician, sorcerer, witch doctor, ascribing to him immense and overarching powers, the kind commonly associated with Greek gods.

> I believe his mind can create things, can make them up as he goes along, real things (so to speak), like this road we were on, or the valley we'd just crossed over, or the mountain above us. If the world is illusion, why shouldn't Gerald be the cause of some of those illusions? I know this sounds insane. I probably am insane. Still and all, can't a madman be logical and right? [175]

The narrator then proposes that Gerald can take the form of birds at night—the demon bird. "Or possibly the crying birds and the baying dogs are in Gerald's pay. They are bribed by him to sound off at the most appropriate moments, when most likely to horrify me." He proceeds to ask whether Gerald, a puppeteer of sorts, might also be responsible for creating the whole setting, including his irritating and inscrutable Moroccan neighbors. Clearly, by this time, Chester was losing his grip. Still, as he himself asks, "Can't a madman be logical and right?"

Chester astutely perceived and articulated the ways Bowles's extended residence in Morocco had transformed him. "Safari" brilliantly displays the relationship between predator and prey. It is all the more poignant when we recall

Paul Bowles, Magic & Morocco

that "Gerald" is none other than the author of "The Delicate Prey" a chilling story in which a young Moroccan is castrated, raped and left for dead—his sting cut from him in much the fashion we see the scorpions tamed. The symbolic potential of the story can be felt strongly. At one point when the narrator realizes that the ground he is standing on might be riddled with literally thousands of camouflaged scorpion holes, he says to Gerald, "Isn't it dangerous with all these scorpions lurking under us?" "Probably," Gerald responds, with a smile, "jiggling."[176]

On yet another level, the story can be read as an allegory of Chester's entire relationship with Bowles. Rather like Arthur Dimmesdale, in Hawthorne's novel, who suspects Roger Chillingworth as the instrument of his increasing mental anguish, Chester was prone to see Bowles as responsible for his suffering. This topic is taken up in the longest portion of dialogue between Gerald and the narrator, at the heart of the story.

Presently, as lightly and casually as I could, I said: "I think I'm being poisoned."

Gerald cupped his hand around his ear. He often likes to pretend he is hard of hearing. "Who?" he said.

"What who? Me!"

"Who are you poisoning?" he asked, looking me full in the face and giving me a flash of all his wicked yellow teeth.

"I'm not poisoning anyone. I think someone is

poisoning me."

"Why, do you feel sick?"

"I feel strange."

"Don't you always feel strange? You always complain about feeling strange."

"I feel stranger than usual."

"But how?"

Of course I didn't want to tell him, for I suspected him of being, if not precisely my poisoner, then certainly involved in my poisoning, in charge of it, as it were, and probably for no better motive than to hear me speak of my reactions. With a big smile, I said:

"Are you poisoning me, by any chance?"

"Me? You're joking, surely."

"Am I?"

"Why on earth would I want to poison you?"

"Why not? Just for fun, I suppose. What else is there to do around here?"

He nodded. "Not much, that's true."

After some silence and a little guilty grief, I said:

"I hope it doesn't offend you, my asking."

He patted me on the back. "Oh, no, not at all."[177]

Chester has perfectly inscribed Bowles's voice and manner here. The paranoia, of course, had been growing ever since he landed in Morocco.

Late in the fall of 1965 Alfred's landlord petitioned the government to have him removed. He somehow slipped out

Paul Bowles, Magic & Morocco

of the country and, by the New Year of 1966, was back in New York, at 71 St. Mark's Place, where, in a rather paranoid-schizophrenic state, he worked on "The Foot." In this extraordinary piece of writing which takes the form of diary entries made over a month from January 31 (1966) to February 26, Chester responds to the brutal, painful rupture of his expulsion from Morocco, the loss of his dogs, the loss of his love, the loss of his paradise, and prays for its return:

> Dear, dear God, give me back my paradise. I am writing this, reader, with the tears falling out of my eyes, for everything was stolen from me. Skoura was murdered. Columbine given to a cop. And Larbi?[178]

Chester's letters to Bowles from this period are marked by the same sparse style and despairing tone found in "The Foot." Typical is one written from St. Mark's Place on March 5, 1966, in which he pleads with Paul, as though praying to the gods, to give it all back to him:

Dear Great Man, Monster,
    whoever you are
    whatever you've done to me,
    you gave me the greatest gift I've ever had, by which I mean, in short, of course, what else, Morocco. Or whatever other name you want to call it.
    Please, Paul, give it back to me again.

I love you as I loved my father whom I hated. But I do love you, because like him you gave me life.

I wish it were three years ago again so that I could know what it was you were offering. Though of course I still don't know.

Could you please like my magic father promise me Morocco again?

I love you and Jane very much.

This letter nakedly enacts Alfred's complicated, conflicting feelings toward Paul. Time and time again he refers to Paul as his "father" whom he loves and hates, his father who has, it seems, been winning the Oedipal battle. Paul "gave" him Morocco and somehow, in Alfred's mind, he was responsible for taking it away, punishing him just as a father would punish a son. Alfred grants Paul the power— the power of the father—to give it all back to him. After all, wasn't Paul the great magician, the sorcerer, the witchdoctor, who could make it all happen, who could transform his life and give him everything he needed to be whole, happy and loved, like the prince or princess in a fairy tale?

Chester returned to Morocco in the spring of 1967 and stayed for around a year before he left once again, perhaps forcibly, after being evicted from the villa he was renting at the base of the Old Mountain in Tangier. And though he tried several times and several ways to get back into the country, he never succeeded. Those gates closed, he decided instead to go to Israel. The day before his departure from France for

Paul Bowles, Magic & Morocco

Lydda, near Tel Aviv, in August 1969, Chester wrote to Paul Bowles, in a large, scrawled hand:

> I am going to Israel tomorrow. I will never forgive Morocco now and probably it isn't important whether I do or not. It is hurting me terribly but I'm just spending huge amounts of money in this hole and I know I will never see you or Tangier again. Maybe Jerusalem is something like Tangier. Maybe I will suffer less and find a place that wants me a little. Paul I will never find again.... It's terrible never to see Tangier again, or Paul or Jane. There is no point going on.... If I never see Tangier again or Paul or Jane, it would be nice they imagine to know how I kiss them and hug them and loved them.

The letter bears neither final greeting nor signature.

Anyway, I look forward to seeing you. You might let me know beforehand just when you'll be arriving. But bear in mind that the post is generally very slow, as is the telegraphic system. It can take a letter a month to get here from the U.S., and a wire a week.
—Paul Bowles to Allen Hibbard, April 24, 1987

Paul Bowles went on living and practicing his magic in Morocco for another three decades after Alfred Chester left in the late sixties. His production slackened as he became older and more sedentary. (It has been suggested that if his life story up to 1970 or so aptly could be titled *Without Stopping*, the last phase of the story could be called *Stopping*.) During this time visitors came and went from the Itesa Inmeuble, like pilgrims at a shrine, each affected one way or another, all returning home with stories of going to Morocco and seeing Paul Bowles.

My own route to Morocco was circuitous. I first came across Bowles unexpectedly, by chance, knowing nothing of him beforehand. One spring day in the early 1980s I was perusing the shelves of the tiny Left Bank Book Store, at the base of Pine Street in Seattle, on the edge of Pike Place Market perched above Elliot Bay. The arabesque design on the cover of a displayed book caught my attention, aroused my interest and curiosity. It was Bowles's *Collected Stories*, recently published by Black Sparrow Press. I bought the volume, took it home, and began at once to read the stories, one after another, propelled by an appetite as intense and insistent as any I had ever felt. I admired the artistry of the stories, the rich, clean texture of the language. The worlds I entered through these fictions were wholly unlike any I had previously known. It was precisely this sense of strangeness, the exoticism, that so seduced and enchanted me. Bowles's fiction fueled a desire for adventure. The writing circulated in my being, like blood, like the air I took in at every breath. I was keenly aware that the writer was still living, unlike Coleridge, Spenser, Joyce and others whose works I was reading in graduate school at the time. After reading first these stories then other works by Bowles, I resolved to go to Morocco, to see if there was indeed a real place like the place in which these narratives unfolded. I determined, moreover, to meet the wizard, to see if I could unveil the secret of his talent, to see if he had a spare pair of magic slippers for me.

I first wrote to Paul Bowles out of the blue, in the early 1980s. It was, I am sure, a silly fan letter. To my surprise and delight, Bowles replied, and we developed a correspondence that continued, intermittently, until his death. It occurs to me now how fortunate I was. Several years later he likely wouldn't have answered. By the time Bertolucci's film version of *The Sheltering Sky* came out in the early 1990s he was enjoying a new surge of fame. Stacks of unopened, unanswered letters accumulated on the floor beside his desk. He simply couldn't keep up with it all.

Now I look back through our correspondence, the slim material traces of intersecting points in our life narratives, points in time. His address (2117 Tanger Socco) remains consistent throughout this period while the array of my addresses suggests a restless nomadism: 50th St. (Seattle), Kasr el-Aini (Cairo), Broadway (Seattle), 215 Maney Ave. (Tennessee), Abu Rumaneh (Damascus), and 312 Maney Ave. (Tennessee). In response to an early letter I wrote expressing admiration for his work, Bowles replied:

> All I can do is thank you for your interest and hope that when you have read more of my work your enthusiasm won't wilt. I wish I could be of some practical help, but I live what might be called a sequestered life here in hope of staying anonymous. It's better that way. (Paul Bowles to Allen Hibbard, 26/x/82)

My enthusiasm didn't wilt, and we continued to exchange words, often about his work. After sharing my responses to the collection of stories *Midnight Mass*, in particular my admiration for "Here to Learn," he replied:

> I like "Here to Learn" best of the *Midnight Mass* volume, myself. I'd always thought of writing such a tale, but didn't get started on it. ("Always" means since 1955, to be precise, when I met Malika.) (The last I

heard of her, she was married to someone in the State Dept., and living outside Washington, D.C., (Paul Bowles to Allen Hibbard, 15/ii/83)

"Please forgive what are visual irregularities you may find in this missive," he wrote at the outset of this handwritten letter. "I'm sick in bed—this is the fourth day, and the fever doesn't budge—remaining at 38 degrees, which is very little, but sufficient to make me insomniac, anorexic and hypersensitive to pain." More and more of his letters were handwritten, as he wrote from bed, unable or unwilling to sit in front of a typewriter.

A year or so later, after hearing a rumor of his death, I wrote first to Joseph McPhillips in Tangier then, later, when I found the rumors were unfounded, to Bowles himself expressing relief that he was still alive. He shot back a postcard with a panorama of Tangier, dated October 6, 1984:

Looking at it from the Moroccan point of view—who invented the curse? For it's true that for the past month I've been nearer to death's door than any previous time in my life. First in a hospital in Switzerland, and then here in Tangier, with scandalously high fever and sweating and shivering. A postcard takes all my energy. I hope to be out of bed in a few days. For to say someone has died is tantamount to expressing the wish for his death. So I say: Who invented the curse? Perhaps some day we'll know.

My first schemes to get to Morocco didn't pan out. While still a graduate student, I applied for a Fulbright, concocting some sort of argument that I needed to go to Morocco in order to understand Bowles's fiction more fully. Truth be told, I simply wanted to get there and hang out. Bowles himself endorsed the plan and even wrote a few words on my behalf, though he seemed a bit bemused by the prospect of someone receiving a grant to come visit him. On January 18, 1983, he wrote, in response to my anxieties about the proposal, "I hope you and the Fulbright come together, even though you say you think it would be foolish of their people to accord you the grant. That doesn't make sense." [179] As I suspected, the Fulbright people didn't buy it.

Way led onto way. Once I passed my qualifying exams, in 1984, I applied for a teaching position at the American University in Cairo, and got it. When I wrote and told Bowles of my plans to go to Cairo, he replied:

> I agree that "it's not Morocco", but Morocco has nothing to compare with the upper Nile, in case one manages to see it. I've never been up the river—only seen Cairo, Port Said and Suez, plus an endless stretch of empty desert, and many palms around Zagazig. I should think it would be worth trying. . . . William Burroughs was here for three days a fortnight ago. I hadn't seen him in years. Since he began to walk with a cane, he finds he can't do without it. (Paul Bowles to Allen Hibbard, 5/ii/85)

Paul Bowles, Magic & Morocco

I'd hoped that somehow I'd get to Tangier from Cairo. The logic wasn't all that crazy, as it turned out. The Director of the Freshman Writing Program at the American University in Cairo, my immediate supervisor, was the British writer Leslie Croxford, whose novel *Solomon's Folly* I read the summer before I left for Egypt, in 1985. Croxford, I quickly discovered, had lived in Tangier in the seventies, and knew Bowles. (Bowles had mentioned in a letter that he knew someone who taught at AUC, though had not supplied a name.) Learning of my interests, Croxford encouraged me to go to Tangier and meet the man myself, offering to write a note of introduction to Bowles and suggesting that I apply for a grant from AUC to finance the trip.

On June 6, 1987 I flew from Cairo to Casablanca, and from there caught a flight on to Tangier. I directed the cab driver to the Atlas Hotel, which Croxford had recommended. The hotel I knew as the place Jane had stayed during one of her periods of exuberant excess, spending money beyond her means. From the balcony of my hotel room I surveyed the city. Antennae sprouted prolifically from the rooftops, as many as twenty, anchored by stays, on one building. The buildings were all square and rectangular, radiant and white in the glaring midday light. The scene became a cubist painting. A wave of doubt and depression came over me, likely because I was suffering from lack of sleep. Tangier seemed far more Western than Cairo. "Why had I come to this city?" I asked myself. "What did I expect to find here?" It seemed, from the outset, that whatever happened to me here could never match the wild, ecstatic transports I had imagined. Perhaps, I thought, I should have left those fantastic constructions intact, pristine, undisturbed. Fiction, after all, is fiction, and I should know well enough not to think that those worlds correspond to anything real. Somewhat dejected, I fell asleep as the muezzin announced the noon-time prayer. When I woke, thirsty, it was already dark. I would have to put off my search for Bowles until the next day.

The Itesa Inmeuble is a modern, four-story concrete apartment building on what was once the outskirts of Tangier. Many have noted, almost gleefully, as though revealing some damning inconsistency or hypocrisy, that a man celebrated for his excursions into the primitive and unknown had chosen such modern, bourgeois digs. I timed my arrival for around four in the afternoon, knowing that this was the time Bowles generally received guests. (He had no telephone.) I roused the concierge, who told me that Señor Bowles was in apartment numero viente. I climbed the stairs to the fourth floor, found the number, and knocked, somewhat nervously. The door was opened by a man I recognized as Mohammed Mrabet, who stood cold and statue-like at the door, like a guard. I told him I was here to see Paul Bowles if this was a convenient time. He admitted me to the tiny foyer. A door to the right opened into a small kitchen. A dozen or so suitcases were stacked against the wall, to the left. Mrabet then parted the curtain separating the foyer from the living room and announced my arrival. Paul was seated to the left, talking to a man about his age. "I am Mohammed Mrabet," Mrabet proclaimed. "And this is Paul Bowles." "Oh, yes. I knew you were Mrabet. And, so you are Paul Bowles?" Bowles chuckled and introduced me to his guest, longtime friend Christopher Wanklyn, a Canadian painter who had once lived in Tangier (in the very apartment we were now in, I later learned) and now made his home in Marrakech. He then welcomed me, asked me about my journey, and told me he had gotten my letter and had stopped by the Atlas two days before to look me up, but that they had no record of me. After polite preliminaries, Paul and Christopher continued the conversation I had walked in on. Christopher had brought back bamboo with him from Japan—miniature bamboo—and planted it in the courtyard of his home in Marrakech. "I thought it wouldn't do any damage, but it's grown so much that the tiles are cracking."

"Couldn't you just pull out the tiles?" Paul interjected, demonstrating a mind ready to handle any practical matter set before him.

"But I like the tiles. And besides, the tiles have to be there. They are part of the house."

As they talked about the tiles, Paul responded in a manner suggesting he pictured clearly every detail of the scene. He listened, drumming his fingers in distinct rhythmic patterns on the arm of the chair beside him.

I left after a brief stay, with an agreement that I would return the next day, at about the same time. On my way back to the Atlas, I reflected on the meeting. I had achieved my goal. I had finally met Paul Bowles. I was not in the least disappointed. I was struck by Bowles's politeness, his manners, his voice, his sense of humor, his charm. This journey now seemed part of a design. It felt so right, so inevitable. Mektoub, as they say in Arabic. It was written. I was simply tracing a pattern that had been etched out before me.

I quickly established my own routine, rising around seven, writing in my journal, taking breakfast around nine, returning to my room to write and read (*Don Quixote*), until two or so, going out for lunch, then visiting Paul. During the evenings I explored the city, indulging in its seedy pleasures, or (when that became boring) staying in my room to work.

9 June 87. Tangier

There is something about this place that is conducive to the establishment of routine. Perhaps it is the city; perhaps it is my discipleship. A major element in Paul's success has been his discipline. There is a sense of routine in the life he lives— and in that routine all needs seem satisfied, appropriately. He writes in the morning. By 2:30 he is ready to receive guests. Abdelouahaid comes by about four and off we go in Paul's old gold Mustang, stopping for the mail, then going to the Fez market. We come back and Mrabet is there and we talk about various *cosas*. . . . Of course, for Moroccans that routine often becomes a routine motivated by survival needs—hustling every day, thinking how to get ten dirhams to buy food.

Paul Bowles, Magic & Morocco

Pilgrimages inevitably take on a similar, archetypal character, affected by topography, by previous stories that wear ruts in the road: all those pilgrims going to Canterbury, or to the Ka'aba at Mecca, performing precisely the same established rituals. I worried that the contours of my experience would be indistinguishable from the pilgrimages of so many fans and sycophants who came to Tangier and called on Paul Bowles.

Gradually, however, the shape of my narrative took on a distinct character. I began to spend more time with Paul; at the same time I was taking in Tangier on my own. A couple of days after my arrival, Paul asked me if I could join him for a walk at 10:30 in the morning. Naturally I was delighted. Soon we were taking walks together every day. One day, on a walk through the Medina, he pointed out the house he once owned there, the one he and Jane finally gave to Cherifa. Another day we stopped by the Fez Market. While Paul was buying soap and shaving cream, the salesman brought out photos of Tagourit. "My favorite quarter of Morocco," Paul told me. "It's like Paradise." The young man asked if I were his son. Paul smiled. "Is there some resemblance?" he asked. As we left, he said, "They see relations everywhere. I bring any European with me and they ask, 'Is this your brother?' 'Is this your daughter?' 'Is this your uncle?'"

One day we walked down to Merkala Beach, past rows and rows of new houses and heaps of garbage that, Paul remarked, had not been there yesterday. He began to reminisce.

"It must be sad to walk through this area and compare

things now and things then," I said.

"Well, I've been living here all the time, so it hasn't happened suddenly. It would be rather shocking if I'd been away and returned."

"Like Malika in 'Here to Learn.'"

"Yes. That's it. She'd been away only a short time and came back and found they'd torn down the old market and everything."

We arrived at the beach, which was swarming with young Moroccans, most of them about ten years old, in skimpy bathing suits. "When we first came here you wouldn't have seen a Moroccan on the beach. Only Europeans."

"Why?"

"They just didn't like the sun. Gradually the younger generation began going to the beach. It was part of becoming modern, imitating the West."

We came across two boys, one who was walking on his hands. Both of us marveled and admitted we could never have performed such acrobatic feats. "Mrabet could, when he was younger," Paul added.

"The Moroccans don't like the trees, many of which the Europeans planted," Paul told me another day, as we were walking up to the Marshan. "They're always cutting them down. They think that evil spirits live in them. And in the hollows of the trees they sometimes place lanterns to collect the evil spirits."

When we got to the top of the hill, not far from Malcolm Forbes's mansion, we took a right, then a left, toward the sea, then another left along a small lane lined with high white walls. There we ducked into a café called Al Hafa ("The Cliff"), overlooking the Straits of Gibraltar. Off the beaten track and unmarked, it was the kind of place one would likely not find on one's own. "Have you ever been here?" Paul asked me, smiling, pleased to be introducing me to a new unforeseen delight. We sat down outside and ordered mint tea. Around us, on several terraces, young Moroccans smoked kif, talked, and played backgammon. There below us the Mediterranean and the Atlantic met. The northwest tip of Africa reached out to touch Iberia. It was truly a crossroads. I recalled the myth of Antaeus, and various associations the name invokes—Bowles's story "Afternoon With Antaeus" and the literary journal he founded: How the legendary Libyan wrestler, son of Poseidon and Gaea, invincible so long as he remained in contact with Earth, straddled the straits, one foot on Europe, one on Africa, until Hercules, seizing upon the famed giant's weakness, lifted him into the air and crushed him. "Fifteen thousand years ago the two continents were connected," Paul remarked. "Fifteen thousand years isn't long, you know. Man was here then." We talked about the end of the 20th century, the systematic devastation of beauty, Mohammed Mrabet, Kurt Schwitters, William Burroughs, Henry James's prefaces, Edith Wharton, Flaubert, writing, painting, Cairo, Tangier, contemporary fiction, his translations, and anthropologists such as Gellner, Westermarck, Geertz, and Crapanzano who had studied Morocco.

At one point, there at Al Hafa, it occurred to me that I now had command of the topography dictating the plot of Bowles's second novel, *Let It Come Down*. "Would that be Jebel Musa?" I asked, indicating a mountain off in the distance to the east, recalling the final sections of the novel when Nelson Dyar and Thami flee Tangier in a launch. "Yes." The novel and its actions thus lay as a palimpsest upon the present scene.

Several days after my arrival, Paul asked me how I liked the Atlas. I told him it was boring, too modern. "I suspect you might like the Continental better. Some people do. It's right at the edge of the Medina, and has more character." That afternoon, on the way to the post office, Paul asked Abdelouahaid to drive down to the Continental. The Mustang barely fit through the narrow street leading up to the gate of the hotel. I liked the place at once. It had an open feel, with an expansive patio looking out over the harbor. A light breeze brushed palm fronds against one another, and carried voices from the medina. Paul took me in and introduced me to Abdelsalaam, the desk clerk, who smiled cheerfully and welcomed us warmly. The ceilings were high, old Moroccan carpets covered the floors, Moorish arches separated rooms. Abdelsalaam showed me a small room with a small desk and small balcony. I determined to move the next day and told him so.

"Would you like to see one of my favorite streets in Tangier?" Paul asked me one afternoon. We got in the Mustang, Abdelouahaid at the wheel, and headed west of town to Monte Viejo, the Old Mountain. Abdelouahaid gunned the engine at the base of the hill and the Mustang shot up the steep, narrow road. I instinctively felt, when we got to the top of the hill, that this was where Paul had written *Up Above the World*. I shared my hunch which Paul confirmed, pointing out the place we were passing on the right, with a view of the Atlantic. "The place has about twenty acres of forest. I walked around a lot. I rented the place for six months—just to write—and kept the flat in town." He also pointed out a large villa where he had lived in 1930 when he first came to Tangier with Aaron Copland. We talked about Conrad (he expressed his admiration for *Nostromo* and *Victory*) and Lawrence (he recommended that I read *Mornings in Mexico* when he learned I hadn't read it). He talked about journeys and books. "Every book, really, is a journey."

One day Abdelouahaid asked Paul if he'd like to drive to his home, near Sebta, about 40 kilometers east of Tangier. Paul agreed and asked if I'd like to go along. (He'd taken a special interest in the place, talking with Abdelouahaid about materials and design, and putting up money.) The next day they came by the Continental to pick me up. The Mustang zipped around the bends of the road as we traversed the hilly coast. We passed by a small old castle where, according to Paul, all the amputated beggars had been taken after Independence. "Nobody knew what happened to them. One day there were no beggars on the streets. It happened over night. And God only knows what happened to them once they were out here."

Purple oleander lined each valley, along river beds. The smell of ripening figs filled the air: "An aroma I shall always associate with Morocco," Paul remarked.

We stopped by a gate leading to a small white house, with fig, pear and olive trees planted on the small plot of land surrounding it. Paul tried to make friends with a goat tied to a pear tree. We stayed for tea and fresh figs before making the return trip to Tangier.

Often Paul and I would have time together in the afternoon before other visitors arrived. One afternoon he put on an old recording of the first movement of his *Concerto for Two Pianos*, then played a piece by Samuel Barber. We talked about composition, musical and otherwise. There are two ways to approach it, he noted. One is to look at what someone else has done and copy the style, substituting one's own notes; the other is to hear the melodies in one's own mind and strike out on one's own. He, of course, chose the latter approach. He heard his own music and wrote it down.

"One of the ingredients of greatness—in art, music or literature—is the development of a personal, recognizable style," Paul continued. We listen and we say that is by so-and-so. We read and we recognize the author's voice and style. "And there is also the matter of invention, taking the form farther than it had been taken before. Then there is influence." He mentioned Wagner, a composer who, though he personally disliked the music (too heavy, too German, too Romantic!), was great, he had to admit, simply because he was so influential. At the heart of genius was the very act of doing, giving form to ideas. One must first create a space to work if there is to be art. "You have to know what you're doing and once you know, then you must be very, very persistent."

One afternoon Paul brought out a copy of an issue of *Twentieth Century Literature* devoted to him and his work. (He diligently read what was written about him.) He read sentences aloud and groaned. "Not only is it wrong, it's badly written!" I found myself wanting to separate myself from this tribe of critics. "At least you're not a biographer!" he told me at one point, as we were discussing the book I planned to write about his stories. He then began to issue complaints about a fellow who had been interviewing him for a biography. When the book finally was published, Paul did not disguise his feelings about the book and its author. "The biography is willfully inaccurate, and in many instances defamatory," he wrote to the editors of *The Boston Globe*.[180] This assessment became the party line.

It occurred to me that I was being tutored (and warned!), that this was my apprenticeship, and Paul was planning out each day's lessons. I was here to learn.

In the afternoons, after the trip to the post office, people would come and go from Paul's apartment, rather like I imagine they came and went from Gertrude Stein's salon in Paris earlier in the century. You never knew who might pop in. There in Paul's living room I met Buffe Johnson, Patricia Highsmith, Rodrigo Rey Rosa, Gavin Lambert, Claude Thomas (Bowles's French translator), Phillip Ramey (a New York composer), and Moustafa Ouaffi (a young Moroccan artist whose paths have since crossed mine most improbably).

Paul received all who came to pay tribute. One day it was a Dutch psychiatrist doing research on Moroccan treatment of abnormal mental conditions. Another: a professor from Notre Dame who claimed to have been good friends with Tennessee Williams. Local musicians came by, as did Englishmen, Spaniards, Japanese— curious tourists or journalists. Mrabet was apt to come in and burst into a tirade against the Jews or against American homosexuals who corrupted Moroccan youth. He praised Moroccans. They were better than all the Arabs—the Saudis, the Egyptians, the Syrians, all of them. They were stronger, more courageous, more faithful to Islam. "And what about the Afghans?" I asked. "Ah, the Afghans! They are something!" He cleared admired how they were fighting the Russians. They were warriors, fierce and fearless. "America is nothing! Yes, they are powerful, but they are empty on the inside. America will fall like other empires. America is decadent!" It sounded as if he'd been reading Ibn Khaldun, the great medieval thinker from Tunisia whose theories of the rise and decline of societies are presented in his classic work *Al Muqaddimah*.

Always Paul was at the center, listening intently to others, nodding, smiling, interjecting a remark, or raising a question. Or, he would tell stories, share anecdotes, gossip. He had a good ear and was an excellent mimic. He was always, as Gertrude Stein said of Pablo Picasso, "one who was completely charming."[181] Though he would frequently complain privately about all the visitors, they sustained and amused him, provided him with an audience, allowed him to keep on being Paul Bowles.

Paul Bowles, Magic & Morocco

In the evening, after the guests left, a few of us (usually Phillip and his friend Kenneth Lisenbee forming the core) would stay on and talk with Paul while his dinner was served. We would sit around his bed—for he ate lying down—and gossip about the people who had come by that day. It felt like a tree house, an airy retreat from that larger adult world below, a free space away from social structures and moral restraint. Phillip was able to pry Paul open like no one else I've seen. Both Paul and Phillip were quick-witted. They loved humor, even (or especially) if it came at someone else's expense. One evening I remember Paul shared a letter from Gore Vidal he'd gotten that day. It began something like "Lennie Bernstein has just been here for four days, which passed with the quickness of a century." Vidal went on with his portrait of the composer/conductor: "He gets up at four o'clock in the afternoon wondering where the sun has gone, then retiring to study Brahms's 2nd and Mozart's 23rd, filling a black hole which might well contain some wit and curiosity." Phillip shared juicy anecdotes about Bernstein. We were all very amused. Paul went on to talk about the nine lives of King Hassan II, how he managed to foil one attempt on his life after another.

This all sounds very pleasant (and it was), yet a sinister quality, a sense of foreboding, lurked beneath the surface. Paul delighted in telling stories that involved terror and violence. Once, I recall, he told of a Muslim man in the Medina who had been living a perfectly normal life, every day carrying a tray of pastries from café to café until one year at *Aid el Kebir*

151

he went to pray at the mosque and came out raving, brandishing two sharp knives. No one dared try to restrain him as he ran wildly through the streets, slashing every non-Muslim in his path. By the time he finally was subdued, he had killed nine people. Walking in the dark late at night through the Medina down to the Continental, I imagined all kinds of gruesome, blood-curdling scenarios. Whether or not there was any rational cause for the fear, or whether it was produced by all of Paul's stories, I can't say.

That first summer I made trips to Fez and Oujda. The following summer I returned to Tangier. "You stayed a very short time this year," Paul wrote to me later that fall (4/x/88). "It wouldn't be any better if you were here now, as practically every day there's someone here trying to squeeze in an interview. French TV comes on Tuesday. I'm told that in the U.S. writers have to spend more time publicizing their works than writing them, so I'm lucky to be here." He was always complaining about these kinds of intrusions, but suffered them nonetheless. "I don't know how people manage to get around me," he once wrote to me (6/iv/86). "I suppose my general tone is not firm enough to drive them away."

Every time I came back to see Paul after being away, he would greet me warmly, as if no time had passed. "Hello, Allen. Where have you been since I saw you last?" And we would pick up where we left off. It seemed as if things would go on like this forever, in a kind of timelessness. I realize now (as I did not then) that I arrived at the last time the going was good. A few years later and Paul would not have been able to walk.

Paul Bowles, Magic & Morocco

He likely would not have been so willing to let someone new into his circle.

Years passed. I returned to Seattle from Cairo, then took a job in Tennessee, then temporarily escaped once again, to Damascus, on the wings of a Fulbright. All the while I kept in touch with Paul. "I hope all is well with you, and that one of these days you'll return here so we can walk in the Medina," he wrote in a letter of July 19, 1991. I told him of my trip to visit the Bowles collection at the Harry Ransom Humanities Research Center in Austin, Texas, where I collected material related to his short fiction and became captivated by Jane's notebooks, containing portions of her unfinished novel, *Out in the World*. Paul wrote back:

> I hope the *Library Chronicle* publishes your piece on Jane's unfinished novel. [It did, in vol. 25, no. 2, 1994.] I don't know how you managed to get anything out of the notebooks. I found them virtually unreadable. So I'm very eager to see what you've written on them.
> ... I also look forward to seeing your book on my short stories, and certainly regret the nuisance for you of getting permission to quote. I wish I could be of help on that, but I don't see how I could be. (Paul Bowles to Allen Hibbard, 14/xi/91)

When my little book on his stories came out in 1993, Paul wrote me a letter with kind words about the book. When he was in Atlanta for an operation, staying with Virginia Spencer

Carr, I went to visit him. I also flew up to New York for the Bowles music festival in 1995 and saw him there.

I didn't return to Tangier until 1997. The stated reason for the trip was to talk to Paul about Alfred Chester for the biography I was writing. More importantly, I wanted to see Paul one more time before he died. By this time he had come to play a significant role in my own life story, and a return at this moment seemed a way of collecting memories, reflecting on them, sealing things up, completing this chapter so I could move on.

It was late evening and wholly dark when the Bismillah ("In the Name of God") docked in Tangier. I lugged my bags, brushing away persistent offers to help from desperate porters and taxi drivers, making my way the several long blocks to the Continental Hotel. There I found everything more or less as it had been a decade earlier. At the gate was Mustafa, who had from time to time helped me procure necessary goods on my earlier visits. "Ah, my friend! You have returned. Life is very good! You are a good man! I stay here and you come back. The world moves on." Abdelsalaam, the perennially cheerful desk clerk, recognized me at once and poured out effusive greetings. Abdellatif, the man who served me breakfast every morning during the summers of 1987 and 1988, wearing (it seemed) the same red fez, white shirt and black Moroccan pants, also greeted me. And the timid maid who had always done my laundry gave me a shy, knowing smile. Abdelsalaam invited me to have mint tea with him. I accepted and sat with him on cushions in the reception room. My cares dissolved.

Paul Bowles, Magic & Morocco

The next day I headed off for the Itesa. I made no wrong turns as I wound my way through the *souq*, up the hill and out past the Spanish Cultural Center. Two monstrous concrete highrises, still unfinished, had popped up on the corner where you turn off to Paul's. First I stopped to see Phillip Ramey, in Jane's old apartment, just below Paul's. For the last decade or so Phillip has divided his time between New York and Tangier. I had timed my arrival so that I could see Phillip before he returned to New York. After a bit of catching up, we went up to Paul's flat. Abdelouahaid welcomed us warmly. (No sign of Mrabet. I later learned there had been a falling out.) To my surprise, Virginia Spencer Carr was also there, scouring the place for letters, notes, scraps of paper that might provide her clues to Paul's life, and checking her facts with Paul.

I walk into Paul's bedroom, where he lies prone, and greet him. We talk about the last time I was there, the walks and drives we took, and where I've been since. He kindly offers me a ginger snap cookie, soggy and near the bottom of a box. I politely decline. At one point he fumbles about trying to find something on the table next to him, cluttered with books, papers, and half-used bottles of medicine. I ask if I can help him with anything. "Could you help me die?" he says, looking up at me with a wry smile. We talk a bit about his being in Tangier at this stage of his life. "Everybody always asks why I'm here. What they don't understand is that I'm a pragmatist. I've lived here so long. Why would I want to go anywhere else, especially now?"

For the most part Paul was bed-ridden. I assumed he was not much heavier than a child, yet his intelligence was perfectly clear, concentrated even. In his shrunken state, he still was in control of all around him. All movement revolved around him. Everyone who was there was there because of him. He held onto the staff even as his voice became fainter, his breathing slower.

For the next several days I divided my time between tracking down Alfred Chester's old haunts, wandering around Tangier, talking with Paul, hanging out with Phillip, Kenneth and Karim, and processing past and present experiences. I readily took Phillip up on his offer to be on hand while I talked with Paul about Alfred. He knew Paul's ways, and Paul was more open and at ease with him than with anyone else with whom I've seen him. There seemed to be no secrets between the two. A few puffs of kif loosened Paul up. The conversation went smoothly. Phillip asked questions I would have thought rather delicate, and would never have had the gumption to ask myself. When Paul became evasive (as he so was prone to do whenever he encountered issues he didn't want to talk about), Phillip would go straight to the point. "It was about sex, wasn't it?" And, after a bit of hemming and hawing, Paul would admit, "Yes, I suppose it was."

When Phillip left, a few days before my own scheduled departure, I felt a little at loose ends. I went out to Asilah, but found no trace of Alfred there where he had lived for some time. I spent more time reading and sleeping. "What am I doing staying in a hotel which has seen better days, in a city

Paul Bowles, Magic & Morocco

which has seen better days, visiting a man who has seen better days?" I wrote in my journal on October 16. "All is in decay." What could I do but wait around until I planned to leave?

18 October

I decide to go to Paul's, since I'm already close by, to say farewell. I knock on the door firmly but not so forcefully that it would rouse him should he be resting. No answer. A young guy who lives in the building comes by, asks in French if I'm looking for Mr. Bowles, and says he's probably out with Abdelouahaid.

Then, later in the day:

> Went back to Paul's. Still no response to my knockings. The thought occurs to me that he could be dead and that perhaps I should take some kind of action to make sure he is all right. But then I think of how Phillip had told me that he had been worried once the past week when Paul hadn't responded to his repeated knockings. It turned out he'd just been asleep, and couldn't hear, with the small fan running on the table beside his bed. I leave a note and choose to let him be. [182]

Now, back here, on the other side, as I think about this last visit, I recall Marlow, wanting to reach the station in the heart of Africa to see and hear for himself the legendary Kurtz before he died. Reflecting on his journey afterwards, while waiting for the tide on the Thames to change, Marlow tried to convey the man's most remarkable qualities to a sleepy audience who had not known the man firsthand. "[O]f all his gifts the one that stood out pre-eminently, that carried with it a sense of real presence, was his ability to talk, his words—the gift of expression, the bewildering, the illuminating, the most exalted and the most contemptible, the pulsating stream of light, or the deceitful flow from the heart of an impenetrable darkness," he told them.[83] And, later: "He won't be forgotten... He had the power to charm or frighten rudimentary souls into an aggravated witch dance in his honor; he could also fill the small souls of the pilgrims with bitter misgivings."[184]

I also recall Paul's own words about death in the final pages of *Without Stopping*:

> The Moroccans claim that full participation in life demands the regular contemplation of death. I agree without reserve. Unfortunately, I am unable to conceive of my own death without setting it in the far more terrible mise en scène of old age. There I am without teeth, unable to move, wholly dependent upon someone who I pay to take care of me and who at any moment may go out of the room and never return. Of course this is not at all what the Moroccans mean by the contemplation of death; they would consider

Paul Bowles, Magic & Morocco

my imaginings a particularly contemptible form of fear. One culture's therapy is another culture's torture. "Good-by," says the dying man to the mirror they hold in front of him. "We won't be seeing each other any more." When I quoted Valéry's epigram in *The Sheltering Sky*, it seemed a poignant bit of fantasy. Now, because I no longer imagine myself as an onlooker at the scene, but instead as the principle protagonist, it strikes me as repugnant. To make it right, the dying man would have to add two words to his little farewell, and they are: "Thank God!"[185]

I'm not interested in immortality. A lot of people are, I know. That's what most religions are about. But all religions are absurd. Immortality is one sliver of their absurdity. They all seem to like the idea of living beyond death. I wonder why. . . . Oh, I'm willing to admit that it's possible that people might remember me for some years after I die.
  —Paul Bowles, *interview with Phillip Ramey, December 1997*

It was Phillip Ramey who broke the news of Paul's death to me. Throughout the day I received dozens of calls and e-mails, from around the world, expressing condolences to me, as though I had lost a loved one or a relative. My sister sent me flowers.

The obituaries summarized Bowles's life narrative and accomplishments, sometimes with a critical edge. David Pryce-Jones, writing for *The Wall Street Journal*, for instance, assails Bowles for the company he kept and laments his waste of talent. "Like courtiers around a monarch in exile, there entered a troop of beachcombers, pimps, parasites, dreamers, worshippers of the Bowles cult, journalists and even a genuine poet or two," he writes, suggesting that Bowles's extended stay in the land of lotus-eaters had resulted in

Paul Bowles, Magic & Morocco

lassitude, a softening of ambition, a dulling of artistic vision. "Impassive, his good looks long since ruined, he allowed this life of kif and stupor to wash over him.... Like a character in his fiction, he had taken steps that could only make him a victim of himself."[186]

In the end, despite all of his insistence that Tangier was his home and he had no desire to live again in America, Paul Bowles did return to his native land for good, though not in a condition allowing for measurement of his cranium to judge just what kinds of changes had taken place in him during his residence in Morocco. In a typical fashion of jesting that contained a good deal of seriousness, Bowles had often told friends that he wished to be buried in the pet cemetery in Tangier. Somewhere, sometime, however, he must have expressed a wish for his body (or remains) to be returned home to the U.S. In a *New Yorker* "Talk of the Town" piece titled "Family Plots: Bowles at Rest," Robert Sullivan recounts the story in a manner similar to Flaubert's narration of "Un Coeur Simple". "What was left of Paul Bowles was his ashes," he writes, "which were being transported to Glenora [New York] in a metal canister by the executor of Bowles's estate, Joe McPhillips."[187] McPhillips, we are told, carried the canister in an L. L. Bean tote bag. There on hand to witness the interment were "friends and neighbors of Bowles from Tangier, a Bowles biographer, a Bowles translator, a Bowles photographer, and a man from Chicago, in a light-gray suit, who claimed to have become a close friend of Bowles in his final years."[188] Those with any knowledge of Bowles's social circle in the last decade of his life would have little trouble identifying the cast of characters from this description: Kenneth Lisenbee, Phillip Ramey, Virginia Spencer Carr, Claude Thomas (I'd guess), Cherie Nutting, and Philip Krone (who read from the Bible at an atheist funeral). The gathered friends touched the canister of ashes before it was lowered into the ground. Then, like at a saint's tomb, each made an offering which was placed in a box McPhillips had brought from Morocco: a handful of soil from Morocco, a tape of his music, a coin, some flowers.

When I told Ira Cohen that Paul was to be buried here in the U.S., not in Morocco, he at once registered shock and dismay, as though this was the ultimate betrayal, a clear sign that Bowles had never really, completely gone over to the other side. After a life playing the role of consummate outsider, the foreigner in an exotic country who had repeatedly chosen exile over return, he had selected as a final resting spot this plot next to his parents, at home. He had not wanted his body to be absorbed by, or eternally committed to foreign soil. McPhillips himself is quoted in *The New Yorker* piece as saying "It's the most barbaric thing he could have done. It's a pain in the ass, for one thing. But it's ironic, and of course he would have liked that. . . . In a way, it's very Bowles!"[189]

Who knows, the gravesite there in Glenora, like Hendrix's in Seattle or Jim Morrison's at Père Lachaise in Paris or Genet's in Larache, Morocco or Jane Bowles's in Málaga, Spain, could become the destination of pilgrims bent on coming in contact with the departed magician's spirit.

These borders between the dead and the living are not hermetically sealed.

—W.G.Sebald

3 January 2002

Dear Paul,

I must confess I miss receiving your letters, addressed in your inimitable, confident hand, with Hassan II stamps and Moroccan postmarks. Death. Must it mean an end to conversation? Who's to say the dead cannot speak across the chasm, the abyss? We, the living, must attend to voices from the other side. Might we not, as Sebald (who himself recently crossed over into the realm you now inhabit) said, have appointments to keep with the dead?

The ultimate death, I suppose, is when people stop talking about you. You have not been forgotten. You live in your music, in your stories. You live in the memories of those who knew you and whose lips still form the shape of your name. People (including yours truly) still write and talk about you.

I don't know what kind of news you've been

receiving lately, so I thought I would fill you in on what has been happening since you died. I know how much you always thrived on news from home. Those trips downtown to the post office, with Abdelouahaid driving the gold '68 Mustang, were always important daily rituals. From my own sojourns abroad I know how those communications with friends from home can be lifelines, holding us in place amidst a culture whose manners and customs are so foreign, sometimes even unsettling. (Letters such as the ones you wrote and received, by the way, are a thing of the past. What we have now is e-mail, faceless electronic communication, composed on and delivered by computers, which I'm sure you would find appalling, another manifestation of the scourge of modernity. No stamps. No envelopes. No time between the sending of a message and its arrival. Hastily written prose with little attention to grammar or style. Even the marvelous rhythm and sound of a typewriter is nearing extinction. But I digress. That is another story.)

The Paul Bowles industry has been humming along nicely since your death. *The New Yorker* continues to run pieces on you from time to time. One was on your burial back in Glenora. (Were you conscious of any of that? Do a person's ashes feel anything?) Another commemorated the publication of the 50th Anniversary edition of *The Sheltering Sky*, brought out by Ecco Press. In the Fall of 2000 the

Paul Bowles, Magic & Morocco

Delaware Library put together an exhibit devoted to your work that originally had been planned to coincide with your 90th birthday. On display were copies of some of your early poems, rare editions of various books, Japanese and Polish translations of *The Sheltering Sky*, copies of sheet music, a typescript of *Points in Time* and various other works with author's corrections, copies of translations of work by Mrabet and others, pages from notebooks, etc., etc. Things you owned, things you touched, things you created, things with your name and signature on them have, like religious relics, become fetishized.

I didn't arrive in time for Virginia's opening address, but did make it to a concert featuring your music. The folks at Delaware are pleased to have so much of your stuff. I guess you worked out a deal with Francis Poole and Tim Murray, the summer before your death, to sell all your remaining papers and, I believe, your library as well, to Delaware. Well, the thirty some odd cartons thankfully, miraculously, made their way from Tangier to Newark. My friend Rebecca Johnson Melvin, a librarian there at Delaware who so graciously hosted me during my visit, asked me to help her identify a few things among their recent acquisitions: A page or two of a typed letter I guessed (correctly as it turned out) was from Irving Rosenthal, and a hastily scrawled note some woman (who seemed infatuated with you) wrote on board a ship. How could I—or anybody else but you—possibly determine who had written it or when? It's strange that your archives have wound up in Newark (pronounced New-Wark, I discovered), Delaware, such a quaint little backwater of a place, with residual airs of a colonial past, such a far cry from Tangier.

I just spoke with Virginia on the phone and she told me she had sent off the manuscript of her biography to her editor at Scribners. It had been a whopping 2,000 pages or so, but they insisted she pare it down. Now it is 978 pages, including around a hundred pages of notes. I've read portions of it at various stages. It will no doubt be a different sort of book than it would have been if it had been published while you were alive. We all remember how much you loved Sawyer-Lauçanno's biography! I know you spent a good deal of time with Virginia the last decade or so. I remember once walking into your apartment and there—to my surprise—she was, ensconced in your study, pouring over papers and looking through your library! Besides the thirteen trips she made to Morocco over eight years, there was the time you were with her in Atlanta after your surgery. So, perhaps she has gotten things right at least. You would learn a great deal about your life from the biography.

Cherie Nutting's beautifully produced coffee-table book with photos and text came out a year or so ago. I presume you knew it was in the works.

Yesterday's Perfume: An Intimate Memoir of Paul Bowles it's called. There are photos of you in the Fez Market, the Continental Hotel, the legendary stack of suitcases in your apartment, Mrabet, Abdelouahaid, you with Mick, you with Ned, you with Virginia, you petting a cat, your typewriter and desk, a pile of mail on the floor, you sitting on the hood of the Mustang, Rodrigo, Phillip, Kenneth, Karim Jihad, Claude Thomas, a birthday celebration, and old pictures of Morocco. There is also a photo collage assembled by Peter Beard. Text by Cherie and portions by you are woven in and around the photos, creating a rich tapestry of your life in the 80s and 90s. Pictures are labeled in your hand, producing the impression of a personal photo album. "It wasn't what Paul said that captured my attention so much as the complete charm of his demeanor," Cherie writes in a caption beside a set of photos of you.

The Library of America is bringing out two volumes of your work, edited by Daniel Halpern, in their prestigious series on American writers. So, you have quickly been canonized and will take your place alongside Henry James, Herman Melville, Sinclair Lewis, Kate Chopin, and others. A fellow named Greg Mullins in—of all places—Olympia, Washington, has just finished a book called *Colonial Affairs: Bowles, Burroughs, and Chester Write Tangier*, which the University of Wisconsin Press will soon publish. And, a fellow from Tunisia named Ridha Trabelsi just sent me a draft of an article he's written on the notion of "alterity" in your fiction. And just yesterday I received an e-mail from a fellow who is trying to put together a panel focusing on your work at the next American Literature Association meeting.

Meanwhile I am working on a little book called "Paul Bowles, Magic & Morocco" for Cadmus Editions. Jeffrey's given me a free hand. No deadlines or anything. After reading a piece I'd written on you and Alfred Chester, he suggested I write something longer, considering you as "a species of North African magician." "One, perhaps the central trope, conceit," he wrote, "ought be the apprehending of genius, a task which is supremely difficult because to apprehend means to enter into, to find the requisite language to describe mental processes which are not ordinary, are extraordinary, beyond the ken of pedestrian language, wot?" He went on: "Should we live to be certifiable old fucks I think such essay might by then have achieved a landmark status—what other figure in American letters might seriously be considered, examined, as a magician? or influenced, sensibility shaped by magic, magic practices? I believe a stunning and important contribution to the discourse on American letters might be added by such work/exploration." With this kind of coaxing, how could I resist? My daughter Alexandra tells me I should stop

Paul Bowles, Magic & Morocco

writing about other people and concentrate on my own stuff. She's right of course. I hope sometime I'll become wise enough to follow her advice.

There is even an International Paul Bowles Society, which I am sure you would find most amusing. Based in London and founded by someone named Josie Farmer (Perhaps you invented Farmer, too?), the society "promotes the works of Paul and Jane Bowles in the written, musical, film, and theatre forms." A year ago last October, the Society sponsored a 22-night tour of Morocco. "During the daytimes, we will have optional (free of charge) Group excursions to the Medinas and other places of interest, such as Museums and Palaces, in each city.... We intend to buy clothes for poor children in each place that we visit and distribute them to those in need.... We will have the Paul Bowles Group meeting each evening, throughout the trip, from 8 pm to 10:00 pm or so, and each of us reads aloud from 'our' book." All in your name! Could you have imagined any of this? I'd love to see your reaction.

The real howler, however, was this admonition: "Please do not apply to join the Team if you are moody, bad-tempered or have any other personality disorders." That would leave out anyone of interest, certainly anyone you ever hung out with, wouldn't it? (No Bill Burroughs, no Jane, no Alfred Chester, no Mrabet, for sure.)

Cherie Nutting apparently now has your old apartment, though her rent is several times what you paid, I'm told. (No wonder you chose not to live in New York or anywhere else in this country, with such cheap rent there in Tangier!) I wonder if you had talked with her about this possibility. I can imagine the thrill she must take living in your old digs, continually reminded of your presence, and telling others that she's now living in Paul Bowles's flat.

Her triumph, as you can well imagine, came none too easily. One Sunday morning over the phone Phillip told me parts of the story. He'd just gotten back from Tangier, where he had gone to help Cherie finalize arrangements for her to assume the lease on the apartment. The flight over was miserable, with insufferable delays. And there were numerous hassles with the Moroccan bureaucracy, of course. As Phillip told the story, however, he focused on Abdelouahaid, to whom, I learned, you'd left all the remaining belongings in the apartment: One last act of generosity to one who had for so long moved freely about your space, preparing meals, doing errands, driving you places, conversing about daily affairs. I remember seeing and talking with him when he accompanied you to the Bowles music festival in New York. I remember how warmly he greeted me every time I came back to Tangier, how fluently the two of you conversed in Spanish, how you showed a real interest in him and his life.

Paul Bowles, Magic & Morocco

Abdelouahaid and Karim were there at the airport to meet Phillip, though the flight was very late. Phillip had $500 in hand for key money to give to Abdelouahaid, insisting that in exchange he take the keys to the apartment. Abdelouahaid seemed uneasy, making excuses for not giving up the keys. "I'll take the money now. You take the keys later." Phillip stood his ground (you know how formidable he can be!) and Abdelouahaid relented, giving up the keys. When Phillip got into the apartment, the reasons for all of Abdelouahaid's hemming and hawing became startlingly apparent. The apartment had been cleaned out! It was completely bare! Abdelouahaid had taken everything, including windows and frames and the hot water heater! When later confronted, Abdelouahaid said that if it hadn't been Cherie who was moving in, he'd have taken the cupboards, the built-in bookcases, and the doors as well.

I suspect you would have simply taken it all in with amusement if you had been there. Things simply are the way they are. Amor fati. I remember you telling (perhaps with a mixture of shock and acceptance of fate) how Cherie entrusted Mrabet with a large sum of money with the understanding that she would get a house out of it. She saw neither house nor money, did she? (Evidently you gave Mrabet a lot of money for the phantom house, too.) There's always a give and take, no? (I can't help thinking of the scene in *L'Immoralist* where Marcel surreptitiously observes

Moktir as he steals a pair of his wife's scissors. The incident thrills him somehow. "When I had given Moktir all the time he needed to rob me properly," Marcel relates, "I turned toward him again and spoke to him as if nothing had happened." You'll recall the scene I'm sure.)

You might be glad you never lived to see the dawn of the new millennium. You thought the 20th century was disastrous, with the two world wars, genocide, the dropping of the bomb, an explosion of population, the plague-like proliferation of hideously designed buildings, and environmental degradation—and you were right, of course. Yet, it seems the world has become an even crazier place since your death. This is the age of terrorism and state retaliation. The rift between the Islamic world and the West has widened dangerously. It has become more difficult than ever to make and hold on to friends on the other side. You know the issues and their history, as you showed in *Points in Time, The Spider's House,* and so many other works. You used to say that World War III would be between the West and the Islamic world, not between the U.S. and Russia. You might not have been so far off. On September 11, this past year two jet planes that had been hijacked and commandeered by Islamic fundamentalists (members of a group called Al Qaida, we are told) were flown into the twin towers of the World Trade Center in New York. The buildings

Paul Bowles, Magic & Morocco

collapsed, dramatically, killing thousands. Another hijacked plane crashed into the Pentagon not more than a half an hour after the first planes hit the towers in New York. CNN caught it all. It was spectacle of the highest magnitude. The images, played over and over again, are firmly embedded in the collective consciousness. Still, for those of us living outside New York, it is hard to conceive of the scope of this tragedy.

The U.S. is now involved in a war in Afghanistan where we have helped topple the Taliban regime (were you alive when the Taliban destroyed the large Buddhist statues?) and are now tracking down a man named Osama bin Laden, a Saudi fundamentalist who, we are told, masterminded these attacks and is thought to be hiding in caves in the Tora Bora region of southern Afghanistan. (We're having a hell of a time trying to find him! We've been looking for four months now!)

Melville foresaw it all, prophetically. In the very first chapter of *Moby Dick* (which I somehow doubt you ever read) Ishmael imagines his own personal odyssey as "a sort of brief interlude and solo between more extensive performances":

> "Grand Contested Election for the Presidency
> of the United States.
> "WHALING VOYAGE BY ONE ISHMAEL
> "BLOODY BATTLE IN AFGHANISTAN."

Allen Hibbard

As Burroughs used to say, what is written will occur. (Oh, you died before the last U.S. election where George Bush Junior, with the help of his brother's attorney general in Florida and his daddy's Supreme Court, managed to win the Electoral College vote while losing to Gore in the popular vote.)

What madness is loose in the world? What beast slouches toward Bethlehem waiting to be born? Writing brings things into the world, gives palpable existence to what was before ethereal, insubstantial, fantasy: Visions of terror as well as visions of bliss. That is the magic.

While all of this has been going on, this past fall a new edition of your stories, *Stories of Paul Bowles*, was published. John Sutherland ends his *New York Times* review of the book with this paragraph: "Paul Bowles had an enviably long life, but one could have wished it at least two years longer. He would, one feels, have had informed things to say about this country's recent agony. Who knows, he might even have dredged up some sympathy."

What have you to say, old sorcerer, with your knowledge of what lies on both sides? Where are you now? What has become of the magic now that you have crossed over to the other side, home of shades? Is the magic dead, too, or has it just moved to another realm, waiting to re-emerge in another place and time, in the form of another life? Speak!

1 Paul Bowles, *Without Stopping* (1972; reprint ed., New York: Ecco Press, 1985), p. 125.

2 *Ibid.*, p. 127.

3 *Ibid.*, p. 128.

4 Dedication to *The Delicate Prey and Other Stories* (New York: Random House, 1950).

5 *Without Stopping*, p. 130.

6 Titus Burckhard, *Fez:City of Islam*, tr. William Stoddart (Cambridge: The Islamic Texts Society, 1992; German 1960), p. 3.

7 *Without Stopping*, p. 149.

8 *Ibid.*, pp. 150-51.

9 *Ibid.*, p. 165.

10 *Ibid.*, p. 366.

11 Washington Irving, *Tales of the Alhambra* (1832; reprint ed., Granada: Marques de Mondejar, n.d.), p. 112.

12 *Ibid.*, p. 113.

13 *Ibid.*, p. 121.

14 Mark Twain, *The Innocents Abroad or The New Pilgrims Progress* (1869; reprint ed. New York: New American Library, 1980), p. 58.

15 *Ibid.*, p. 66.

16 Paul Bowles, *The Sheltering Sky* (1949; reprint ed. New York: Ecco Press, 1978), p. 14.

17 Pierre Loti, *Morocco (Au Maroc)*, tr. W. P. Baines (1889; New York: Frederick A. Stokes Co., n.d.), p. 177.

18 *Ibid.*, p. 5.

19 *Ibid.*, p. 2.

20 *Ibid.*, p. 6.

21 *Ibid.*, p. 19.

22 *Ibid.*, p. 14.

23 *Ibid.*, pp. 138-39.

24 *Ibid.*, p. 228.

25 *Ibid.*, p. 325.

26 *Ibid.*, p. 326.

27 *Ibid.*, p. 327.

28 *Ibid.*, p. 327.

29 Typescript of nine interviews with Matisse conducted by Pierre Courthion in 1941, Archives of the History of Art, Getty Center of Art and Humanities, Los Angeles, quoted in Pierre Schneider, "The Moroccan Hinge," *Matisse in Morocco: The Paintings and Drawings, 1912-1913* (Washington, D.C.: The National Gallery of Art, 1990), p. 36.

30 *Matisse in Morocco*, p. 31.

31 Archives Charles Camoin, quoted in *ibid.*, p. 32.

32 *Morocco*, p. 18.

33 It might be noted in passing that Picasso's trips to Spain from Paris in the early part of the 20th century also seemed to have acted as a catalyst, leading to more modern stylistic innovations. In her sweet little book *Picasso*, Gertrude Stein writes, "Once again Picasso in 1909 was in Spain and he brought back with him [to Paris] some landscapes which were, certainly were, the beginning of cubism." (Boston: Beacon Press, 1959, p. 8; first published in French by Librairie Floury in 1938).

34 Quoted in Schneider, "The Moroccan Hinge," *Matisse in Morocco*, p. 31.

35 Edith Wharton, *In Morocco* (1920; reprint ed., New York: Hippocrene Books, 1984), p. 28.

36 *Ibid.*, p. 11.

37 *Ibid.*, p. 36.

38 *Ibid.*, p. 44.

39 For a thorough discussion of Lyautey's influence within the context of the development of Moroccan cities, see Ron Messier and Jim Miller, "Historic Preservation in Morocco: Questions from Fez and Sijilmasa" (unpublished manuscript). Under Lyautey, they note, "policies were established to delineate separate socio-cultural spheres, European and Moroccan, that would serve to preserve the Moroccan cities, the medinas, from the sudden and dramatic French economic development of their new 'protectorate,' as Morocco was called. Thus, modern cities or *villes nouvelles*, grew up alongside the old cities which "were fossilized, in many ways, leading to their present condition as spectacular images of the past—preserved, despite their underlying problems of having become the residence of the displaced poor with ever-higher population densities and relatively weak infrastructures of every modern type." Messier and Miller conclude: "We have, ultimately, Lyautey and his broad grasp of the wealth of Moroccan life to thank for the purity of their survival, so clear in their structural and visual qualities, in contrast to the many traditional cities despoiled

by modernization strewn elsewhere across the map of North Africa and the Middle East" (pp. 6-8).

40 Edward W. Said, *Orientalism* (New York: Random House, 1978), p. 6.

41 *Ibid.*, p. 20.

42 *Ibid.*, p. 23.

43 Any such account would no doubt consider works such as Lawdom Vidon's *Tangier: A Different Way* (Metuchen, N.J., 1977), John Maier's *Desert Songs: Western Images of Morocco and Moroccan Images of the West* (Albany: SUNY Press, 1966), and *Mirrors on the Maghrib: Critical Reflections on Paul and Jane Bowles and Other American Writers in Morocco,* ed. R. Kevin Lacey and Francis Poole (Delmar, NY: Caravan Books, 1996).

44 I took up the question in a paper "Paul Bowles's Fictional Images of North Africa: Orientalist?" presented as a part of a panel on "Imagining North Africa" at the 2000 Middle East Studies Association convention. See also: Ralph Coury, "Paul Bowles and Orientalism," in *Mirrors on the Maghrib*, pp. 199-225, and Timothy Weiss, "Paul Bowles as Orientalist: Toward a Nomad Discourse," *Journal of American Studies of Turkey* 7 (Spring 1998), http://www.bilkint.edu.tr/~jast/Number 7/Weiss.html.

45 Edward Said, *Beginnings: Intention and Method* (New York: Basic Books, 1975), pp. 318-19.

46 Edward Westermarck, *Ritual and Belief in Morocco*, 2 vols. (London: Macmillan and Co., 1926), 1:18.

47 *Ibid.*, 1:21.

48 *Ibid.*, p. 19.

49 *Ibid.*, p. 26.

50 Westermarck, *The Belief in Spirits in Morocco*, Acta Academiae Aboensis, vol. 1, no. 1 (Finland: Abo Akademi, 1920), p. 121.

51 Alfred Bel, *Pour une Enquête sur les Survivance Magico-Religieuses en Afrique du Nord* (Extrait du *Bulletin de l'Enseigement des Indigènes de l'Academie d'Alger*: Alger, 1936), p. 1.

52 Nina Epton, *Saints and Sorcerers: A Moroccan Journey* (London: Cassal, 1958), p. 33.

53 *Ibid.*, p. 44.

54 *Ibid.*, pp. 44-45.

55 *Ibid.*, p. 45.

56 *Ibid.*, p. 171.

57 *Ibid.*, p. 62.

58 *Ibid.*, p. 117.

59 Vincent Crapanzano, *The Hamadsha: A Study in Moroccan Ethnopsychiatry* (Berkeley: University of California Press, 1973), pp. 32-35.

60 Clifford Geertz, *Islam Observed: Religious Development in Morocco and Indonesia* (New Haven: Yale University Press, 1968), p. 44.

61 *Ibid.*, p. 44.

62 Mircea Eliade, *Rites and Symbols of Initiation: The Mysteries of Birth and Rebirth*, trans. Willard R. Trask (New York: Harper & Row, 1958), p. 95.

63 *Ibid.*, p. 102.

64 In an e-mail message dated 5/31/02 2:58:59 Pacific Daylight Time,

and titled "Further Thoughts from the Insomniac Theatre," Jeffrey Miller notes that "one aspect of Paul's fascination with magic and the total sensorium was his assiduous collecting of scents, his collection of such things, various forms, liquids, perfumes, crystals, resins, grains, from various parts of the world. Don't know if you visited during the winter but Paul would, sometimes, after the fire had burnt down, a bed of red coals, throw things onto the coals which would subtly scent the air. Sometimes he would do this openly, offhandedly comment on such, other times, if observed carefully, he would do this surreptitiously."

65 Personal journal, Tangier, June 14, 1987.

66 Quoted in Jeffrey Miller, "Preface," *In Touch: The Letters of Paul Bowles* (New York: Farrar, Straus and Giroux, 1994), p. vii.

67 Lesley Chamberlain, *Nietzsche in Turin: An Intimate Biography* (New York: Picador, 1998), p. 25.

68 Arthur Rimbaud, *Illuminations*, tr. Louise Varèse (New York: New Directions, 1957), p. 67.

69 Paul Bowles, *Their Heads Are Green and Their Hands Are Blue: Scenes from the Non-Christian World* (1972; reprint ed. New York: Ecco Press, 1985), p. 129.

70 Ira Cohen, "Interview with Paul Bowles, 1965," in *Conversations with Paul Bowles*, ed. Gena Dagel Caponi (Jackson: University Press of Mississippi, 1993), p. 17.

71 Jeffrey Bailey, *The Paris Review*, no. 81 (1981); reprinted in Caponi, *Conversations*, pp. 130-31.

72 *Ibid.*, p. 131.

73 Michael Rogers, "Conversations in Morocco," *Rolling Stone* v. 161 (May 23, 1974); reprinted in Caponi, *Conversations*, p. 79.

74 Cohen, "Interview with Paul Bowles," p. 24.

75 Paul Bowles to Peggy Glanville Hicks, November 5, 1951, *In Touch: The Letters of Paul Bowles*, ed. Jeffrey Miller (New York: Farrar, Straus and Giroux, 1994), pp. 242-43.

76 Paul Bowles, quoted in Millicent Dillon, *A Little Original Sin* (New York: Holt, Rinehart and Winston, 1981), pp. 157-58.

77 Jane Bowles, letter to Paul Bowles, undated (likely summer of 1948), Harry Ransom Humanities Research Center, University of Texas, Austin, quoted in Dillon, *A Little Original Sin*, p. 161.

78 Accounts of these interactions can be found in Christopher Sawyer-Lauçanno, *An Invisible Spectator: A Biography of Paul Bowles* (New York: Weidenfeld & Nicolson, 1989), p. 317, and Dillon, *A Little Original Sin*, pp. 254-55.

79 Paul Bowles, in interview with Michael Rogers, Caponi, *Conversations*, pp. 82-83.

80 "The Cherifa Plant," in Cherie Nutting with Paul Bowles, *Yesterday's Perfume: An Intimate Memoir of Paul Bowles* (New York: Clarkson Potter, 2000), p. 59.

81 *Ibid.*, pp. 60-61.

82 *Ibid.*, pp. 62-63.

83 Cited in *An Invisible Spectator*, p. 334.

84 *Ibid.*, p. 334.

85 Paul Bowles to Virgil Thomson, Aug. 31, 1957, *In Touch*, p. 273.

86 Vincent Crapanzano, *Tuhami: Portrait of a Moroccan* (Chicago: The University of Chicago Press, 1980), p. 102.

87 *Their Heads Are Green*, p. 116.

88 Brion Gysin, *The Last Museum* (New York: Grove, 1986), pp. 167-172.

89 Gore Vidal, *The Golden Age* (New York: Random House, 2000), pp. 456-57.

90 William Butler Yeats, "Magic," *Essays and Introductions* (New York: Macmillan Co., 1961), p. 41.

91 *Ibid.*, p. 43.

92 *Ibid.*, p. 28.

93 *Ibid.*, p. 41.

94 Cited on Web site: www.cix.co.uk/~mandrake/crowley.htm.

95 Lawrence Sutin, *Do What Thou Wilt: A Life of Aleister Crowley* (New York: St. Martin's, 2000), p. 7.

96 *Ibid.*, p. 180.

97 Writers of the 18th and 19th century, of course, also depicted encounters between the "civilized" and the "primitive." Especially notable are Herman Melville's fictionalized travel narratives featuring Westerners in the South Sea Islands. In *Typee*, for instance, conventional connotations of the two opposing terms are called into question, if not in fact reversed. "Melville's idyllic South Sea setting is a backdrop to a bountiful satire of some of the most sacred aspects of civilized life, foremost among them being religious, sexual and military practices," I write in a discussion of the novel ("Some Versions of Ironic (Mis)Interpretation: The American Abroad," *Alif* (Journal of Comparative Poetics), Cairo, no. 8, Spring 1988, 67-87).

98 Marianna Torgovnick, *Gone Primitive: Savage Intellects, Modern Lives* (Chicago: University of Chicago Press), p. 8.

99 Malinowski, quoted in Westermarck, *Ritual and Belief*, p. 21 fn.

100 Joseph Conrad, *Victory* (1915; reprint ed. New York: Penguin, 1963), p. 21.

101 *Ibid.*, p. 86.

102 *Ibid.*, p. 167.

103 *Ibid.*, p. 33.

104 D.H. Lawrence, *Mornings in Mexico* (1927; reprint ed. New York: Penguin, 1986), p. 12.

105 *Ibid.*, p. 9.

106 *Ibid.*, p. 72.

107 *Ibid.*, pp. 54-55.

108 *Ibid.*, p. 74.

109 *Ibid.*, p. 75.

110 *Their Heads Are Green*, p. vii.

111 Bowles's contributions to ethnomusicology are just beginning to be appreciated. The Library of Congress houses hundreds of tapes Bowles made of musical performances throughout Morocco. Some of this music can be found on *Jilala* reissued by Akasha and *Morocco: Crossroads of Time*, produced by Randall Barnwell and Bill Lawrence, released by Ellipsis Arts.

112 *Their Heads Are Green*, pp. 27-28.

113 Paul Bowles, *Let It Come Down* (1952; reprint ed. Santa Barbara: Black Sparrow Press, 1980).

114 The Cuban writer Alejo Carpentier's marvelous novel *The Lost Steps* (1953) lends itself to remarkable comparisons to Bowles's life and work. The narrator, a composer, tires of life in the modern metropolis and goes off to the jungles of South America with his mistress in search of primitive cultures whose rudimentary musical instruments might provide proof to his theories on the origins of music. (*The Lost Steps*, tr. Harriet de Onís, Minneapolis: University of Minnesota Press, 2001.)

115 *Their Heads Are Green*, p. 184.

116 Norman Mailer, "Evaluations: Quick and Expensive Comments on the Talent in the Room," *Advertisements for Myself* (New York: Perigree Books, 1959), p. 429.

117 William S. Burroughs notes this connection between rock and Moroccan trance music in "Rock Magic," an article on Led Zeppelin featuring an interview with Jimmy Page. "The Led Zeppelin show depends heavily on volume, repetition, and drums. It bears some resemblance to the trance music found in Morocco, which is magical in origin and purpose—that is, concerned with the evocation and control of spiritual forces. In Morocco, musicians are also magicians. Gnaoua music is used to drive out evil spirits. The music of Joujouka evokes the God Pan, Pan God of Panic, representing the real magical forces that sweep away the spurious. It is to be remembered that the origin of all the arts—music, painting, and writing—is magical and evocative, and that magic is always used to obtain some definite result." (William Burroughs, "Rock Magic: Jimmy Page, Led Zeppelin and a Search for the Elusive Stairway to Heaven," *Crawdaddy*, June 1975, p. 35.) When Burroughs pointed out to Page these connections between Moroccan trance music and rock, the rock star readily acknowledged the connections, saying that regrettably he had never been to Morocco.

118 D.H. Lawrence, *Psychoanalysis and the Unconscious* and *Fantasia of the Unconscious*, intro. Philip Rieff (New York: Viking, 1960), p. 45.

119 D. H. Lawrence, *The Plumed Serpent* (1926; reprint ed. New York: Vintage, 1959), p. 113.

120 A recent, interesting manifestation of the phenomenon is the documentary film *Keep the River on Your Right: A Modern Tale of Cannibalism*. Filmmakers David and Laurie Gwen Shapiro retrace the excursions of Tobias Schneebaum, a New York Jewish anthropologist who in the sixties fled the city and traveled through the jungles of the Amazon basin in Peru and Irian Jaya, Indonesia. As he returns to these places decades later, the large, affable, balding anthropologist looks into the camera and reflects upon his earlier experiences. He admits to suffering from alienation and a desire for purer, less complicated relationships with men. He is shown sitting in a canoe, smiling, wearing a yellow plastic poncho, his wide eyes aglow, his arm wrapped round a former lover, whom he has remarkably found, alive and well, though aging too, on his return to the tropical islands. Gleefully Schneebaum recounts how his primitive friend has a string of male lovers in various surrounding villages. Schneebaum blows the gaff on anthropology, openly displaying the deeply personal motives behind his travels. His wish is not merely to observe the natives, but literally to embrace them.

121 Joseph A. Boone, "Vacation Cruises; or, The Homoerotics of Orientalism," *PMLA* 110: 1 (January 1995), p. 89.

122 *Ibid.*, p. 90.

123 William Burroughs, *The Letters of William S. Burroughs 1945-1959*, ed. Oliver Harris (New York: Penguin, 1994), p. 197.

124 Paul Bowles, "Ahmed Yacoubi As Painter," *Nexus* 33 (1998), p. 105.

125 Greg Mullins, *Colonial Affairs: Bowles, Burroughs, and Chester Write Tangier* Madison: The University of Wisconsin Press, 2002.

126 Charles Baudelaire, "The Poem of Hashish," in *My Heart Laid*

Bare and Other Prose Writings, trans. Norman Cameron (London: Soho, 1986), p. 77.

127 *Ibid.*, p. 77.

128 Paul Bowles, Cadmus' 2 lp phonodisc *Paul Bowles Reads A Hundred Camels in the Courtyard*, 1981 and republished in CD versions issued by Cadmus Editions and Dom America, 1999. Republished as Preface, *A Hundred Camels in the Courtyard* (San Francisco: City Lights, 1981; originally published in 1962).

129 *A Hundred Camels, ibid.*, p. 57.

130 Paul Bowles, "The Worlds of Tangier," *Holiday* 23 (March 1958), p. 66.

131 Richard F. Patteson, *A World Outside: The Fiction of Paul Bowles* (Austin: University of Texas Press, 1987), pp. 129-130.

132 Paul Bowles, "The Frozen Fields," in *Collected Stories 1939-1976* (Santa Barbara: Black Sparrow Press, 1979), pp. 261-276.

133 *Without Stopping*, p. 20.

134 *Ibid.*, p. 21.

135 *Ibid.*, p. 27.

136 Gena Dagel Caponi, *Paul Bowles: Romantic Savage* (Carbondale: Southern Illinois Press, 1994), p. 16.

137 *Without Stopping*, p. 66.

138 *Ibid.*, p. 195.

139 *Ibid.*, p. 267-68.

140 These translations and others are collected in *She Woke Me Up So I Killed Her*, trans. Paul Bowles (San Francisco: Cadmus Editions, 1985).

141 *Ibid.*, pp. 261-62.

142 Recounted by Yeats in "Magic," pp. 38-40.

143 Paul Bowles, *Collected Stories*, pp. 407-8.

144 Similarly embued with magic are stories recorded by Leonora Peets, an Estonian woman who went to Morocco with her physician husband in 1929, settling in Marrakech and staying on for forty-five years [Leonora Peets, *Women of Marrakech: Record of a Secret Sharer, 1930-1970*, tr. Rein Taagepara, intro. Stephen W. Foster (Durham, N.C.: Duke University Press, 1988)]. Nowhere have I seen analysis of Peets and Bowles, though their parallel residencies in Morocco and their respective productions make the two ripe for comparison. Peets's stories, as the title of the collection suggests, are especially noteworthy for the entry they provide into the lives of Moroccan women. In a piece entitled "Couscous of the Dead" (more reportage than fiction), Peets tells of various episodes involving digging up graves and using corpses for various supernatural purposes. At the center is the story of Lalla Hedda who learned the ways of witchcraft from her foster-mother, whose chest contained "potent materials like aloe and myrrh for subduing spirits, and coreander and leather shavings for conjuring demons. It also contained human hair, bits of nails, and urine—and even more efficacious ingredients out of which Tammou knew how to brew a sensational love potion by adding the right amount of finely-pestled Spanish flies" (40). Lalla Hedda, a waif and orphan, falls in love with a handsome young man next door. The romance seems off to a propitious start until the young man inadvertently comes upon Lalla Hedda and her foster-mother in a cemetery where they had dug up the grave of a recently deceased bride and were using the dead body to prepare a magical couscous concoction for a client. The discovery abruptly puts a halt to the relationship.

145 Westermarck, *Ritual and Belief*, p. 49.

146 *Ibid.*, p. 48.

147 *Ibid.*, p. 48.

148 *Collected Stories*, p. 375.

149 Paul Bowles, *Midnight Mass* (Santa Barbara: Black Sparrow Press, 1981), p. 129.

150 Mohammed Mrabet, *Love with a Few Hairs*, trans. by Paul Bowles (London: Peter Owen, 1967). p. 12.

151 *Ibid.*, p. 14.

152 Mohammed Mrabet, *The Chest,* trans. by Paul Bowles (Bolinas: California: Tombouctou Press, 1986), p. 86.

153 Paul Bowles, *Days: Tangier Journal: 1987-1989* (New York: Ecco, 1991, p. 26.

154 Raphael Aladdin Cohen, "Paul Bowles and the Spider," *Nexus* vol. 33, no. 2 (Winter 1998), p. 100.

155 *Without Stopping*, p. 48.

156 *Ibid,* p. 49.

157 *Ibid.*, pp. 49-50.

158 Alistair Graham, with illustrations by Peter Beard, *Eyelids of Morning: The Mingled Destinies of Crocodiles and Men* (Greenwich, CT: New York Graphic Society, Ltd., 1973), p. 11.

159 *Ibid.*, p. 68.

160 *Ibid.*, p. 80.

161 Edward Field, "The Mystery of Alfred Chester," *Boston Review*, March/April 1993, p. 16.

162 Edward Field, telephone conversation, March 5, 1998.

163 Edward Field, quoted in John Strasbaugh, "A Charming Monster's Comeback," *New York Press* 24-30 October, 1990, p. 9.

164 Special Collections, University of Delaware Library.

165 Alfred Chester to Edward Field, August 14, 1963.

166 Alfred Chester to Edward Field, July 11, 1963.

167 Alfred Chester to Harriet Sohmers, July 20, 1963.

168 Alfred Chester to Edward Field, March 10, 1964.

169 Alfred Chester, "Safari," in *Head of a Sad Angel: Stories 1953-1966*, ed. Edward Field (Santa Rosa: Black Sparrow, 1990), p. 233.

170 *Ibid.*, p. 234.

171 *Ibid.*, pp. 240-41.

172 *Ibid.*, pp.235-36.

173 *Ibid.*, p. 241.

174 *Ibid.*, p.242.

175 *Ibid.*, p238.

176 *Ibid.*, p.241.

177 *Ibid.*, pp. 237-238.

178 Alfred Chester, " The Foot," in *Head of a Sad Angel*, p. 255.

179 *In Touch*, p. 150.

180 Published in *The Boston Globe Magazine,* Sunday, July 15, 1990; see *In Touch,* p. 543.

181 "Picasso," in *The Selected Writings of Gertrude Stein,* ed. Carl Van Vechten (Random House, 1972), p. 333.

182 "Tangier Revisited: A Diary" *Nexus* 33:2 (Winter 1998), pp. 120-21.

183 Joseph Conrad, *Heart of Darkness* (1899; reprint ed. New York: W. W. Norton, 1988), p. 48.

184 Ibid., p. 51.

185 *Without Stopping,* p. 367.

186 David Pryce-Jones, "A Nihilist's Wasted Talent," *The Wall Street Journal,* November 23, 1999, p. A22.

187 Robert Sullivan, "Family Plots: Bowles at Rest," *The New Yorker,* December 11, 2000, p. 43.

188 *Ibid.,* p. 44.

189 *Ibid.,* p. 43.

ABOUT THE AUTHOR

Allen Hibbard's personal narrative inscribes a trajectory of movement between the United States, the Middle East and North Africa. From Washington State he went off to college at American University in the District of Columbia. He veered off to Egypt in 1985 where he taught four years at the American University of Cairo and wrote his dissertation, "Writing Differently Somewhere Else: Studies in the American Expatriate Novel," with a view overlooking the Nile. Several years later he was to be found in Syria where he was a Fulbright lecturer in American literature at Damascus University. His reviews, essays, and translations have appeared in numerous journals; he is currently teaching, writing a biography of Alfred Chester and translating, with Osama Isber, *A Banquet of Seaweed,* by the Syrian novelist, Haydar Haydar.

ABOUT THE ILLUSTRATOR

Hermann Nitsch, who was born in Vienna, rose to prominence during the sixties as a founding member of the Viennese Action Artists. Thereafter his reputation continued to grow as he took his own performance art actions from Austria to Germany, the United States and Italy. In 1971 he purchased Castel Prinzendorf, the home of his Origen Mysterien Theater, where in 1998 he staged his gesamtkunstwerk, "The 6-Day Play in Prinzendorf." Nitsch has also gained international renown as a painter, graphic artist, musician and writer. He has been a professor at the Academy of Visual Arts (Stadelschule) in Frankfurt since 1989. Nitsch's paintings and graphics are in both private and public collections throughout Europe and North America; his work has been exhibited in the Musuem of Modern Art, New York; the Guggenheim Collection, New York; University Museum, Yale University; Tate Gallery, London; Musèe Centre Georges Pompidou, Paris; Museum Moderner Kunst-Stiftung Ludwig, Vienna; Museum Ludwig, Cologne; Lenbachhaus, Munich, Staatsgalerie, Stuttgart.

ABOUT THE TYPE

Cadmus Editions is honoured to be debuting Richard Whitney Beatty's digital version of Elzevir, called Elzevirs, based on Linotype Elzevir and Monotype Cadmus Old Style No. 22.

D. B. Updike tells us, "Elzevir, the other great name in the history of printing in the Netherlands, belongs properly to the seventeenth century. The founder of the family, Louis Elzevir, a bookseller and bookbinder at Louvain, removed to Leyden for religious reasons— the Elzevirs were Protestants—in 1580, and began to publish books there ... and for nearly a century and a half they were the best known printers of the Low Countries, who published editions of the classics in convenient form.

"The Abbé de Fontenai, writing in 1776, says that the Elzevirs 'have made Holland celebrated for printing, through an elegance of type which the most famous printers of Europe have never been able to attain, either before or since. The charm consists in the clearness, delicacy, and perfect uniformity of the letters, and in their very close fitting to each other' and he adds that 'the taste of young people for literature very often shows itself by a great fondness for these little Dutch editions, which give so much pleasure to the eye.'"

Most of the punches for Elzevir were cut by Christoffel van Dijk.

This
first edition
of *Paul Bowles,
Magic & Morocco*,
printed for Cadmus Editions
by McNaughton & Gunn in April,
2004, consists of a trade edition in wrappers
and 50 numbered copies in boards
signed by the author and illustrator. Composed and
set in Richard Whitney
Beatty's *Elzevirs*.
Design by
Jeffrey
Mill-
er